A PLAN FOR THE ABOLITION OF SLAVERY

Josiah Wedgwood, Cameo

ca. 1790

A PLAN FOR

THE ABOLITION OF SLAVERY

CONSISTENTLY WITH THE INTERESTS

OF ALL PARTIES CONCERNED

BY

MOSES E. LEVY

EDITED WITH AN INTRODUCTION BY

CHRIS MONACO

WACAHOOTA PRESS

Micanopy • Florida

Portions of the Introduction appeared earlier in an article by the editor in the journal *American Jewish History,* published by The Johns Hopkins University Press, and are used by permission.

Library of Congress Control Number unk82084930
ISBN 0-9653864-0-6

Introduction

MOSES ELIAS LEVY published *A Plan for the Abolition of Slavery* anonymously in London in 1828. At first glance, Levy's life appears to be enveloped in contradictions: Jewish colonizer and former arms dealer, frontier settler and urban sophisticate, radical religious reformer and biblical conservative—these apparent incongruities continue to hinder any facile definition of his beliefs. Perhaps the most glaring manifestation of Levy's dual nature was his status as slave holder and ardent abolitionist. The fact remains, however, that Moses E. Levy of Florida—one of the few Jewish plantation owners in the entire South—was the author of an abolitionist pamphlet published during an extended stay in London. This work was released in England shortly before Levy's final return to the United States and, despite contemporary references crediting him as the author of such a plan, the publication never surfaced again, until now.[1] *A Plan for the Abolition of Slavery, Consistently with the Interests of All Parties Concerned*—long held as an anonymous tract in the British Library and the Library of Congress—not only serves to clarify many apparent discrepancies but also gives much needed insight into the life and motivations of this industrious and fervently religious man.[2]

Levy conducted his abolitionist activities at a time when anti-slavery issues were identified with the Evangelical Movement of the Church of England and such Dissenters as Methodists, Quakers, and Baptists. Consequently, his was the only Jewish-American voice amid an

Introduction

outpouring of Protestant fervor in England. Levy's outspokenness placed him at odds with the Anglo-Jewish establishment. An outsider not bound by a strict sense of public reticence, he openly challenged both the Evangelical assumption of moral leadership in social reform and the Anglo-Jewish ideal of assimilation. Levy's denunciation of slavery and his advocacy of a "gradualist" approach to emancipation also serve to contradict previous assertions that "there was not a single abolitionist among the Jews of the South."[3]

The proof for Levy's authorship of *A Plan for the Abolition of Slavery* rests on a number of facts, the most apparent is the time and place of publication. As historian Jacob Toury has noted, 1828 was the year that Levy promised "to publish a plan for the abolition of negro slavery throughout the world" while in London.[4] On August 28, 1828 Levy delivered a copy of his "pamphlet on the Slave question" to an acquaintance.[5] Since the anonymous tract is dated July 1, 1828—the timing is impressive. To further strengthen the case, on July 9, the weekly London religious newspaper *The World* announced the release of *A Plan for the Abolition of Slavery* in an editorial.[6] The newspaper described the author as a man "possessed of a great benevolence of soul, and a deep and enlightened piety." Numerous letters written by Levy were published in *The World* and his activities—including abolitionist lectures—were well known to the readership. Several months prior to the publication of the pamphlet, the paper acknowledged Levy by name and noted his religious piety and benevolence. Significantly, not only do the date and place of publication match, but the editors of *The World* exhibit a personal knowledge of the unnamed author when they attest to his moral and religious integrity.[7]

A Plan for the Abolition of Slavery reveals a depth of personal experience that narrows the possibility of authorship to a select few and coincides, to a remarkable degree, with Levy's own personal history. The pamphleteer admits that he resided "in slave-holding countries for more than twenty-four years . . . under peculiarly advantageous circumstances."[8] This length of time corresponds precisely to Levy's residence in St. Thomas, Puerto Rico, Cuba, and finally, Florida. Furthermore, a review in the London *Literary Chronicle* specifically mentions that the "author has lived 20 years in the West Indies."[9] Again, this very exact reference agrees with Levy's arrival in St. Thomas in 1800 and his final departure from Cuba to the United States in 1820. For much of this period Levy held a lucrative and powerful position as an arms and munitions supplier to the Spanish colonies, owning a fleet of commercial sailing vessels.[10] His business also led him to South America during the turbulent time of Simon Bolivar's wars of independence.[11] Accordingly, many of the pamphleteer's first-hand accounts focus on the Spanish colonies of the Caribbean and South America and also offer a brief commentary on Bolivar. These countries were intensely restrictive to outsiders, especially non-Catholics and most particularly to Jews. San Juan, Puerto Rico, during the early part of the 19th century, has been described as a "garrison town with a siege mentality. It feared not only foreigners but even the inhabitants of the rest of the island."[12]

Moses Levy's fluency in Spanish and his special and unique friendship—beginning in 1812—with the Intendant of Puerto Rico and later Superintendent of Cuba and the Floridas, Don Alejandro Ramírez, allowed him uncommon privileges in the areas of Spanish control.[13] He became Ramírez's chief contractor and principal agent in bolstering the moribund Puerto Rican economy.[14] As a result of his singular importance, the laws of the Inquisition were suspended, and Levy became the first professing Jew to own a sugar plantation on the island and was even allowed to observe the Sabbath by closing his counting house on Saturdays.[15] Levy was also on equal terms with the affluent planter and merchant class in Cuba—where he later moved—and could have easily described in detail, as the pamphleteer does, a meeting among the most "opulent" planters on the island that took place "in the year 1812 or 13."[16] It is extremely unlikely that either a Protestant or another Jew could have participated in many of the scenes described by the pamphleteer—especially during these years. It wasn't until 1817 that the economic reform policies of Ramírez opened Cuba for the first time to foreign merchants.[17] Levy's position, therefore, was unparalleled and quite different from those who would arrive later.

Introduction

Further evidence appears in the author's word choice and in the promotion of specific philosophical ideas. The pamphlet's dedication to "The Religious Public" and its appeal to "those persons who both acknowledge *and feel* the influence of Divine Revelation" bare a striking resemblance to Levy's writing style.[18] Although the unnamed author frequently uses Evangelical terminology, there is not a single reference to Jesus Christ. Instead, the pamphleteer, like Levy, makes a significant effort to create a common moral ground among all people, regardless of religious denomination.

The concept of man's universality was near and dear to Levy. Additionally, his characteristic interest in public education—a revolutionary idea at the time—and the inclusion of the Bible as the centerpiece for all education are important components of Levy's world view. His condemnation of classical Greek and Latin writers as "heathens" was certainly in stark contrast to the high regard most educators held them in.[19] Similarly, the pamphleteer makes known his aversion to "classical" studies when he addresses the education of the children of slaves.

> Give the child an opportunity of coming within the influence of the word of God and the secrets of nature, uncontaminated by studies of heathen morality, and he need not apply to the classical scholar to teach him wisdom, taste, or even refinement . . . To understand, and to be trained to act up to the dictates of the Bible, and the easy and simple knowledge of nature, is, and ought to be the patrimony of every person.[20]

The following excerpt from Moses Levy's May 28, 1828 lecture to a meeting of Christians and Jews contains the same basic premise:

> Was it not absurd to suppose, that after casting the mind into the mould of Heathen principles . . . that the principles of revelation would have their due effect, in producing obedience to the will of God? In the schoolroom, Homer, Virgil, Ovid . . . and the like, were the instructors of the youthful mind, in temporal matters and the principles of taste; and on his entrance into the world, the Bible was presented to his acceptance, for the purpose of spiritualising the principles previously generated.[21]

Introduction

In further stating his case for the corrupting influence of "classical education" Levy specifically warns of its deleterious effect on people and their inevitable assumption of certain character faults—specifically, "emulation, ambition and vain-glory."[22] Most impressive is the pamphleteer's choice of words in presenting the exact same concern when persons are "moulded" by a non-religious education. The results are: "self-love, ambition, vain-glory, and the like."[23]

There are numerous other items of similarity that exist between the *Plan for the Abolition of Slavery* and the writing of Moses Elias Levy. But what of the overall picture that the parts present? The unnamed author is extremely well-traveled, and had a first-hand knowledge of not only the Caribbean and Central and South America but the entire eastern seaboard of the United States as well. He is intimately familiar with sailing vessels and their manufacture. The author advocates a simple agricultural life, free education for all children regardless of sex or financial circumstance, and the importance of following only the literal word of the Bible. He is a utopian by nature, and did not hesitate to envision the formation of societies on a global scale, communities whose real allegiance is to God and not to nations. In essence the broad picture matches Moses Elias Levy's own unique background and stated goals.

The question may arise, however, as to which Bible the pamphleteer is referring to. As previously noted, Levy promoted the use of the Bible in meetings before Christians and Jews, so its subsequent recommendation in the treatise is not inconsistent with his beliefs. Since he also believed in the separation of Jewish life and identity from any non-Jewish country in which they happened to live—he desired to found a separate Jewish colony—the recommendation of an essentially Christian lifestyle for the children of slaves was a recognition on Levy's part that Gentiles shared the values and traditions of the Old Testament, which he believed was the literal word of God. He was never in favor of conversion.

The case for Levy's authorship is strong, but the question of his choice of anonymity still remains. Anonymous tracts were not uncommon during the early nineteenth century. If one considers that Levy's main ambition was to reach beyond his circle of supporters and to affect social change on a mass scale, his identification as a Jew would have been a hindrance. In correspondence dated 25 years later a greatly embittered Levy describes an episode in England regarding his daughters. He states that ethnic prejudice "obliged [them] to take feigned names at the Brighton school."[24] Within the European context England was a comparatively liberal society; however, strong anti-Semitic sentiment still pervaded the culture. In 1828 English Jews could not vote, hold public office, attend universities, or, with the exception of physicians, enter the professions.[25] Since anti-slavery issues were hotly contested among all classes of British society, Levy would certainly want the merits of his arguments to stand on their own, without religious bias.

It also should be noted that if Levy's name had ever appeared on such a pamphlet and been discovered in Florida, where he was already labeled by some as "a man of eccentric ideas," he would have been quickly branded as an abolitionist.[26] This was, apparently, not an option he wanted to endure and he succeeded in keeping his anti-slavery views out of public in the U.S.. His advocacy of intermarriage between whites and blacks also would have placed him in direct conflict with statutes in East Florida which prohibited any such contact and inflicted stiff penalties against whites who transgressed the law.[27] In short, the ideas Levy espoused in London would certainly be viewed as revolutionary and dangerous in East Florida and would have further jeopardized his cherished settlement plans.

Levy became a U.S. citizen after he arrived in Florida in 1821. His life in the West Indies had allowed him a first-hand knowledge of the brutal nature of slavery not only as practiced by the Spanish but also the English, French, and Danish. Levy's early origins also provided a global perspective that would influence his later convictions. Born in 1781 in Morocco to an influential Jewish courtier of Sultan Sidi Muhammad, Moses' privileged life abruptly ended after the death of the sultan resulted in a nationwide anti-Semitic rampage.[28] At age nine he fled with his parents to the safety of British Gibraltar where a traditional Sephardic education awaited him. Given the tumultuous nature of his childhood it is not surprising that as a teenager in 1796 he became deeply depressed.[29] Writing much later he attributed this state of mind to the "doctrine of materialism" which was presented to him by a visiting French relative. Despondency was followed by an intense spiritual catharsis inside a Gibraltar synagogue where he experienced pain "surpassing the idea entertained of hellfire," an event which led to a renewed commitment to his faith.[30] During this episode (similar to the conversion experience common to Evangelical Christians) Moses Levy "swore never to doubt the Bible."[31]

Levy's father died while in Gibraltar and this misfortune, coupled with a widespread epidemic, forced the family to seek better prospects abroad.[32] In 1800 Moses arrived in the Danish Virgin Islands with his mother and infant sister.[33] In a few years, at 22, he married Hannah Abendanone, the daughter of one of the respected Jewish families on St.Thomas.[34] After some lean financial years he managed to save $3,500, which he invested in a lucrative lumber business, becoming a partner in the firm of Levy, Benjamin and Robles.[35] (His partner, Philip Benjamin, is the father of Judah P. Benjamin, U.S. Senator and Confederate Secretary of State.)[36] Later, in Puerto Rico, he became a major contractor to the Spanish army. When his friend Alejandro Ramírez was transferred from Puerto Rico to Cuba as Superintendent, Levy—recently separated from his wife—followed.[37] As a young father of four, Levy had already filed for divorce on the grounds of mutual incompatibility.[38] His son David, who would eventually become a United States Senator, later attributed his parents' divorce to his father's "peculiar [religious] views."[39] Eventually he amassed a considerable fortune. A desire to establish a refuge for persecuted European Jews in the United States would lead him to forsake his West Indian commercial interests, a momentous decision that would affect the course of his remaining life.

In 1820, while in Havana, Moses Levy purchased 53,000 acres in Spanish Florida with the expectation that it would be ceded to the United States. Shortly after, he visited the U.S. and made his plans for a religious colony known to the Jewish leadership in New York,

Introduction

Philadelphia, and Norfolk. By 1821 Levy's idea of creating an agricultural colony became linked with the establishment of a Hebrew school that he called a *Chenuch* or Probationary.[40] This school was intended for the "education of Hebrew youth of both sexes." In addition to religious instruction and courses in "the useful arts and of science," students would also be instructed in "lessons of agriculture." Joining Levy's endeavor were Mordecai Noah, Judah Zuntz, and the Reverend M. L. M. Peixotto of the Hebrew Society of New York. It is clear, however, that this group preferred a settlement "in a healthy and central part of the Union," not the tropical climate of Florida.[41] Levy was willing to give up everything in Florida if the settlement/school was to actually proceed. Interest in the scheme appears to have waned, however, and although Noah did purchase some land in the area of Levy's Florida settlement, Levy ended up financing the entire project alone.[42]

He proceeded with the arduous task of creating a viable sugar plantation, with various dwelling houses, a sawmill, a blacksmith shop and by a road linking his holdings to the St. Johns river—a substantial achievement by itself.[43] By 1824 Levy had spent a vast fortune but few Jewish settlers actually arrived at his Pilgrimage Plantation in the north Florida settlement of Micanopy.[44] Before leaving for Europe, he put Frederick S. Warburg, a relative of the famed Jewish banking family from Hamburg and one of the first Jewish settlers in Micanopy, in charge of the plantation's accounts and supply stores.[45] Levy arrived in England in 1825 with hopes of persuading affluent members of the Jewish community to contribute to his cause.[46] While he ultimately failed in this regard he clearly excelled in his newfound role as ardent proselytizer during these London years. His intimate familiarity with slavery as it existed in various forms throughout the world gave him a breadth of knowledge that few abolitionists could claim.

Moses Levy had strong family ties in England, where he sent both his daughters and his eldest son for their education. In addition, it is likely that Samuel Yuli—the business representative of the Sultan of Morocco who lived in London—was a close paternal relative.[47] Aside from immediate family, however, Levy's exact familial connections in

Introduction

England are not known. Shortly upon arrival one of his first efforts to garner support for his Florida Jewish colony was a letter addressed to Isaac Goldsmid, the first hereditary Jewish baronet in England and, later, a leader in the movement for Jewish emancipation.[48] In this letter Levy disassociated himself from the well-publicized attempt by his former colleague, Mordecai Noah, to set up his own "Ararat" colony for European Jews in upstate New York, a debacle which did not generate a single settler. He dubbed Noah's efforts "folly and sacrilegious presumption."[49] Nevertheless, Levy's appeal went unheeded.

Levy traveled six times between America and Europe during this period; in 1826, while in Paris, he mortgaged some of his Florida land holdings.[50] Returning once more to London and taking up residence in the fashionable neighborhood of Knightsbridge, Levy captured public attention by delivering numerous lectures to a variety of reform-minded organizations, including the Philo-Judean Society.[51] England was undergoing profound social and cultural changes during this period, and many educated citizens took particular interest in the Jews and sought to learn more about the Hebrew religion and language. Considering the long history of anti-Semitism and the continued inability of Jews to achieve full rights of citizenship, this sudden candor—limited though it was—represented a revolutionary turn of events. As one clergyman from Bristol remarked, "This excitement and these discussions between Jews and Christians are certainly extraordinary signs of the times and shew that something most singular is approaching."[52] Indeed, the status of most Anglo-Jews was still marginal at best, and the majority were relegated to the peddler class. Living in the West End of London with its facade of Georgian respectability, Levy was also deeply concerned about the degradation of his people, most of whom lived in tenement squalor in the East End. Within this polarized culture he seized every opportunity to promote his notions of a just society.

While Levy's efforts to attract Jewish colonizers to Florida continued, most of his energy seems to have shifted to participating in open dialogues with Christian activists, not only among the Philo-

Judeans but also among the more aggressive (in terms of conversion activity) London Society for the Promotion of Christianity among the Jews.[53] Significantly, these Protestant activists were also staunch abolitionists. Membership of the London Society included such notables as William Wilberforce, Zachary Macaulay, Charles Simeon and other prominent abolitionists known as the Clapham Sect.[54]

The praise thrust upon Levy by Evangelicals was in stark contrast with the low regard they held for Anglo-Jewry as a whole. Most Jews had grown lax in their orthodox religious beliefs, and the practices of the Jewish elite were not any better. Although wealthy individuals, such as the Goldsmids, frequently held high offices within their congregations, they were more inspired to establish social equality with the Protestant gentry than with any adherence to orthodox religion. According to Todd Endelman, historian of the Georgian period, "Anglo-Jewry as a whole was not characterized by either its piety or its learning," and this secularization among all classes was "without parallel in the Jewish world of the time."[55] He attributes this breakdown in orthodoxy to the lack of traditional social and religious institutions that otherwise would have enforced conformity. As in the United States, most Jews were relative newcomers, and strong communal bonds did not exist.

By comparison, Moses Levy must have shone like a light in the wilderness. Here was a fervently religious Jew who was not only conversant in the ancient language and observed the Sabbath but also believed in strict adherence to the Old Testament.[56] Therefore he personified, in the Evangelical view, a pure form of the Hebrew religion, the wellspring from which Christianity had sprung.

Although Levy believed that the Bible was the revealed word of God, his antipathy to rabbinical teaching and to the Talmud makes any assumption about his religious beliefs especially difficult. It seems, however, that Levy was influenced by a small, radical branch of Reform Judaism—originating in Germany—which had just begun to appear in England during the 1820s.[57] Reform Judaism challenged rabbinical authority and advocated universal concepts such as the brotherhood of man and individual responsibility.[58] Such liberal

Introduction

political and spiritual ideas allowed Moses Levy to cross over religious lines and to partake in discussions with Christians, even dedicating his abolitionist pamphlet to the "Religious Public."

Levy's temperament coincided with the Evangelicals to a remarkable degree. They both idealized ancient Israel, which Levy particularly cherished as his lifelong model for utopian speculation.[59] In addition, one of the Evangelicals' main attributes was a strong activist spirit. Activism was especially apparent during the British anti-slavery crusade, where "propagandists . . .raised anti-slavery sentiments almost to the status of a religion."[60] Slaves eventually enjoyed emancipation in the British colonies between 1833 and 1838 after reform laws cleared the way for a Whig majority in Parliament. After a hard-won victory by a broad coalition of activists, England could justly feel a sense of moral leadership regarding slavery.

Considering the formidable obstacles of prejudice, it was a significant event when "Moses E. Levy of Florida" became a respected name in reform circles. His notices and published speeches in *The World* earned him a remarkable degree of celebrity.[61] In lectures before the Philo-Judeans and other groups Levy also demonstrated an impressive knowledge of scripture, frequently incorporating Hebrew passages in speeches and serving as a quasi ambassador for the Jews (making certain it was understood their "discussions [were] as moralists rather than religionists.")[62] Additionally, a lengthy correspondence with the Englishman John Forster was published—at Levy's suggestion—shortly after his return to America in a book entitled *Letters Concerning the Present Condition of the Jews*. Levy inspired another publication, *Letters to the Jews: Particularly Addressed to Mr. Levy of Florida*, by Thomas Thrush, which included the full text of a speech—described by Thrush as "extraordinary and impressive"—by Moses Levy at a meeting of Christians and Jews in 1828.[63] In July of the same year *A Plan for the Abolition of Slavery* was released. The London *Literary Chronicle* recommended it "to the serious attention of the legislature and the public."[64]

While most of the anti-slavery rhetoric of the day consisted of impassioned arguments for outlawing an oppressive institution, Levy was unique in advocating a position that included broader economic issues.[65] He emphasized the development of nonslave-dependent agriculture and the chartering of companies to implement these changes. "Such is the plan," he states, "offered to the consideration of those actuated by principal, and not by feeling, and are willing to do more than meet and pass condemnatory resolutions."[66] Levy drew upon his own background as a plantation owner in Cuba and Florida to formulate his plan for the demise of slavery. Implicit in his vision was a gradual rather than an immediate end to a system he also believed "diametrically opposed to the Bible".[67]

Further, he was convinced that abrupt freedom would result in even greater harm. "My opinion is that mankind generally fail in their projects, by endeavoring to sow and to reap before the proper time and season."[68] By 1828, however, public sentiment in England—as well as with abolitionists in the United States—began to shift away from gradualism to swift emancipation.[69]

British public opinion notwithstanding, the *Literary Chronicle's* recommendation of Levy's treatise to the legislature is of particular interest because in 1828 Parliament was controlled largely by West Indian plantation owners and their allies. To these slave holders a moderate, long-term approach would probably elicit interest—despite Levy's pessimism that the "West Indian nabobs" would "raise a clamor against the system" until experience convinced them otherwise.[70] At the same time his pamphlet was released an organization was formed which reiterated many of the points Levy formulated in his tract. It is likely he played a major role in the creation of "The Society Formed for the Purpose of Abolishing Slavery throughout the Civilized World." The Society met every Friday night at Salvador House, Bishops Gate, one of Levy's main venues on the lecture circuit.[71] *The World* outlined several of the organization's tenets:

> the Society shall endeavor to obtain a Charter from the British government for the establishment of agricultural plantations in the British colonies under a system of agriculture adapted to free labor . . . and the children of the Negroes belonging to the Society shall be placed on an

Introduction

establishment separate from their parents under a system of education which shall be based on Holy Scripture; that they shall be instructed on the principals of agriculture and trained to such other pursuits as shall be deemed beneficial and obtain their freedom at the age of 21 years, receiving from the Society the provisions above prescribed for emancipated slaves. [72]

Although there is no record of the Society actually implementing any of these goals, this declaration restates several of Levy's key provisos, including his recommendation—albeit indirect—of a Protestant religious education for the children of slaves (referred to in his tract as "practical religion"). He stresses that this instruction in the "pure word of the Bible" would not be for "faith only, but the regulation of their conduct."[73] Throughout *A Plan for the Abolition of Slavery*, the broader terms of *Revelation* and *Providence* as well as quotes from the Old Testament, are used in lieu of specific references to Christianity. Universal access to education was one of Levy's guiding principals, and his trust that "useful knowledge" would elevate the status of slaves to freemen was in keeping with reformist expectations.

Despite the ease he felt in Evangelical religious circles (including shared terminology and ideals), it would be incorrect to assume that Moses Levy was in any way proassimilationist in regard to the status of Jews. Another aspect of his paradoxical nature was that he would always remain a staunch separatist. Colonization efforts in the United States were the result of a conviction that "no amelioration can be expected at the hands of nations for us; on the contrary, the nations of the earth expect their amelioration at our hands."[74] In contrast, Levy's abolitionist strategy advocated the eventual mixing of whites and blacks through miscegenation, a concept apparently inspired during his days in Cuba and Puerto Rico, where racial intermingling was common. Equally liberal views apparently did not extend to his own people. "The race of the Jews has miraculously been continued unmixed with the people of the nations through which they have been scattered."[75] He even issued a blunt warning to those who merely desired full integration into society: "Every Jew who contributes knowingly to the . . . amalgamation of the House of Israel is an enemy to his nation, to his religion, and consequently, to the world at large."[76]

Also inherent in Levy's outlook was a fervent antinationalism.[77] This predisposition can be seen in his Plan when he advocates the establishment of a "United Association" as "the best and most effectual means of annihilating the slave trading system."[78] Such a noteworthy and idealistic concept would be in opposition to an emerging British nationalism–a force that some scholars believe was an unspoken corollary of the moral and religious tenets of English abolitionists (as well as missionaries).[79] Abolition as cultural imperialism does not entirely explain Levy's motives, however. As a practicing utopian colonizer of the early nineteenth century, his Universalist tendencies were perhaps more in line with Robert Owen (the British textile magnate turned utopian socialist) than the Clapham Sect, who, for all their reformist outcries, kept themselves safely within the ideological and political boundaries of the Church of England. Levy, on the other hand, actively sought to "establish colonies of 'Harmonites' upon utopian principles."[80] In the case of his proposed "association," a reliance upon the unity of nations "to destroy that inhuman traffic" was admirable, but since Britain's leadership in the abolitionist cause became identified with national virtue, His Majesty's Government was not likely to subordinate these ambitions to any international authority.

Another unique feature of Levy's plan is his advocacy of the diversion of British convicts to the West Indies or Latin America, rather than Australia.[81] Once the convicts were settled, Levy theorized that intermarriage with the resident slave population would be of immense value in reducing the polarity and inherent conflict among the races.

The spirit of the black population will be thus neutralized, and, by attending to the education of their freeborn offspring, the now wild wastes of America will be populated by an enlightened generation, in which the black skin will be lost with slavery in the gradual shades of improvement.[82]

Aside from the inherent racist views indulged in by Levy—albeit with the higher motive of emancipation—penal transportation itself would prove to be a dismal failure. It should be noted, however, that in 1828 the institution was still generally seen as a progressive step in criminal justice, and the horrors of the journey to New South Wales were either suppressed or ignored. Since it was regarded as "wise and humane," a reformer such as Moses Levy would naturally consider the merits of transportation within his own ambitious scheme. The degree of misinformation in the newspaper accounts that Levy cites, which speak of the desire of ordinary men for the "free passage to a good country," is of course ludicrous in respect to the abhorrent conditions all convicts suffered. [83] It is ironic that the evils of West Indian slavery were better known in England than the equally abusive realities of transportation, which continued under the guise of "enlightened policy." Despite the lack of knowledge and the cultural prejudices regarding prisoners in general, Levy exhibits a highly paternalistic attitude toward crime and punishment. Concluding that "the place of banishment is no longer a dread," he proposes "that crime will receive some check from the dread of transportation to a climate considered unhealthy, which, with the horrors of West Indian slavery, will operate more powerfully on the mind than even the fear of death."[84] To add to this miserable scenario, freedom would not be an option for either slave or criminal in his lifetime. It would be a right reserved only for the succeeding generation.

There is no doubt that Moses Levy possessed an austere outlook in much of his writing, although this rigidity was tempered by sincere humanitarian impulses. While engaged in trade, his cross-cultural experiences made him keenly aware of the "prejudices of the white against the black; and the corresponding hatred it engenders in the breast of the black."[85] As a result, he remained pessimistic in regard to their immediate liberty. He was also convinced that "the vengeance of retributive justice" would emerge if slavery was allowed to continue and he cites the bloody uprisings of Haiti as proof of impending danger. Thus, he appeals to the self-interest of the slave owner, rather than using only moral arguments.

Shortly before the release of *A Plan for the Abolition of Slavery* Levy wrote to John Forster, with whom he had been conducting a long theological debate, that "I have been, and still am unwell, both in body and mind."[86] This brief personal comment, so much in contrast to the more formal, but enthusiastic nature of their correspondence, could very well have been the result of news from America—bad tidings indeed. Indian unrest, lack of business profits, scarcity of settlers, even the questionable validity of his land holdings, bought while Florida was still under Spanish dominion—all these difficulties foreshadowed even bleaker times for the cosmopolitan reformer. Three months later he moved from Park Row, Knightsbridge to the area of the Old Bailey and presented Forster with a copy of his "pamphlet on the slave question," confiding that he was much hurried, "being on the eve of my departure for America."[87] After 1828 he would never return to England or to the Continent.

Levy continued to reside in Florida until his death in 1854. In contrast to his prodigious reform activities in London, his Florida years were marked by numerous financial difficulties. Nevertheless, Levy was active in territorial affairs, helping to organize the first free school and, in the 1830s, serving on a legislative committee which sought to establish an "academy or seminary of higher learning."[88] Abolition, of course, was not a topic which could be safely broached in the Deep South. Levy's activities in the North would also have been curtailed, since any reports could very well have been carried by newspapers throughout the country. Therefore, *A Plan for the Abolition of Slavery*—the first publication written by a Jewish citizen of Florida—was kept safely undercover as an anonymous work.[89] Levy, always fond of agricultural metaphors, would surely have viewed the entire effort as sowing the seeds, while others reaped the harvest of his righteous labor. While his serious work toward abolition still remains unknown in Florida, perhaps his greatest legacy was the spirit of philanthropy and humanism that he brought to the territory—a distinction that various writers attributed to him throughout the nineteenth century.

Levy was one of only a handful of Jewish plantation owners in the South.[90] As was the custom, his sugar plantation relied on slave labor—an economic necessity of the time which troubled Levy greatly. In fact, his pamphlet emphasized the vital need to develop nonslave dependent agriculture,"particularly with respect to raising sugar."[91] He believed that the ownership of slaves should be universally banned in "50 or 100 years." Before that date slaves, through no fault of their own, would be compelled to endure their lot in life because the institution itself had corrupted their "nature." A provision for the separate education of the children of slaves would enable the next generation to achieve freedom. This approach—however moderate it appears today—aimed at the elimination of one of the plantation economy's prime tenets, making Levy unique among the plantation owners of the South. He was also a rarity among Jews. According to Bertram Wallace Korn, American Judaism "had not yet adopted a 'social justice' view" during the antebellum period and the "Talmudic maxim that 'the law of the land is the law [for the Jews]'" was still the norm.[92] At a time when American Jews were striving to conform to the dominant values held by the larger society in which they found themselves, the sentiments that Levy espoused remain a startling and singular achievement.

In December 1835 Moses Levy suffered a severe setback when his beloved Pilgrimage Plantation was burned by Indians at the onset of the Second Seminole War.[93] It was the final blow to his Jewish settlement efforts in Florida. The Panic of 1837 and subsequent bank failures further eroded his financial resources, and he lived the rest of his life in St. Augustine. For many of these years Levy endured real poverty and was $50,000 in debt.[94] His dire circumstances led him to periods of depression, but his deep faith allowed him to prevail. "I have to be thankful," he wrote, "for the want and misery I suffered . . . Thus situated—my soul being saturated with the object of the call of Israel."[95] Toward the end of Levy's life, a court settlement finally allowed him to sell off a portion of the 100,000 acres of land which he had accumulated.[96] Thereafter, he paid off his debts and still left a sizeable inheritance at his death.[97]

Regardless of Levy's misfortunes as a planter and colonizer, he clearly excelled in his role as moralist. Unfortunately, none of his children shared his beliefs. In the case of his youngest son, Senator David Levy Yulee, proslavery conformity and disassociation from Judaism were the ultimate rebukes to his father's lifelong dedication to reform. As easily as Levy perceived the corruptible nature of slavery and its negative influence upon members of his own family, he could not prevent its ultimate ascendancy, especially in regard to David's beliefs.[98] David Yulee became one of the most influential figures in the state. The years of alienation between father and son raise the sad possibility that Levy's staunch religious and abolitionist beliefs spawned the exact opposite effect in his strong-willed son and contributed instead to the unbending character of the antebellum states-rights warrior nicknamed the "Florida Fire Eater."

Moses Levy's abolitionist record also stands in stark contrast with the proslavery views of his onetime associate and failed Jewish colonizer, Mordecai Noah. It is doubtful the two ever reconciled. However, Levy did find certain acceptance within the Jewish leadership in the U.S. and maintained correspondence with such well-known persons as Rebecca Gratz of Philadelphia.[99] In 1830 his unprecedented experience in England was recognized by the prominent New York physician Dr. Daniel Peixotto who introduced Levy as follows: "The transactions of the Philo-Judean Society possess great interest, and for the independent stand which he took in the long neglected cause of his people, Moses E. Levy, Esq., of Florida, whom I am pleased to call my friend, deserves the gratitude and love of his brethren."[100]

Introduction

Endnotes

1. References to Levy's pamphlet can be found in Levy to Forster, 28 August 1828, and Forster, preface, in John Forster and M. E. Levy, *Letters Concerning the Present Condition of the Jews: Being a Correspondence between Mr. Forster and Mr. Levy* (London, 1829), vi and 83.

2. Levy believed in the Divine authority of the Hebrew Bible. It should be noted that he was not "devout" in the typical orthodox sense, since he rejected Oral Law .

3. Bertram Wallace Korn, *Jews and Negro Slavery in the Old South–1780-1865* (Elkins Park, PA., 1961), 64.

4. Jacob Toury, "M.E. Levy's Plan for a Jewish colony in Florida:1825," in *Michael, On the History of the Jews in the Diaspora*, ed. Lloyd P. Gartner (Tel-Aviv, 1975), 25.

5. M. E. Levy to John Forster, 28 August 1828, in *Present Condition of the Jews*, 83.

6. *The World* (London), 9 July 1828.

7. Ibid.

8. [M. E. Levy], *A Plan for the Abolition of Slavery, Consistently with the Interests of All Parties Concerned* (London, 1828), 3.

9. Quoted in, *The World* (London), 20 August 1828.

10. M. E. Levy, letter to the editor, *Florida Herald and Southern Democrat (St. Augustine)*, 23 January 1843.

11. "Certificate of Don Julian Fernandez de Rodan and Don Claudio Martinez de Pinillos," 23 August 1820, (Havana, Cuba), in *Florida Herald and Southern Democrat (St. Augustine)*, 11 January 1843.

12. Rene Velazquez, "The Intendancy of Alejandro Ramierez in Puerto Rico" (Ph.D. diss., University of Michigan, 1972), 2.

13. M. E. Levy, letter to the editor, *Florida Herald and Southern Democrat (St. Augustine)*, 1 February 1843.

14. Ibid.

15. Ibid.

16. [Levy], *Abolition of Slavery*, 19.

17. M. E. Levy, letter to the editor, *Florida Herald and Southern Democrat (St. Augustine)*, 23 January 1843. Ramírez's transformation of the economy of Puerto Rico earned him the position of Superintendent of Cuba and the Floridas. See Velazquez, "Alejandro Ramírez," 214-15.

18. [Levy], *Abolition of Slavery*, 30.

19. "Lecture of Mr. Levy of Florida at a Meeting of Jews and Christians," *The World* (London), 28 May 1828, in Thomas Thrush, *Letters to the Jews; Particularly Addressed to Mr. Levy of Florida: with a Copy of a Speech, said to have been delivered by him, At a Meeting of Christians and Jews, In London, In May, 1828* (York, 1829), 99-104.

20. [Levy], *Abolition of Slavery*, 30.

21. "Lecture of Mr. Levy of Florida at a Meeting of Jews and Christians," *The World* (London), 28 May 1828, in Thrush, *Letters to the Jews*, 101-2.

22. Ibid., 101.

23. [Levy], *Abolition of Slavery*, 26.

24. M. E. Levy to Rachel [Levy] Henriques, 1 September 1853, Yulee Papers, P. K. Yonge Library of Florida History, University of Florida, Gainesville, Fl. (hereafter cited as PKY).

25. Mel Scult, *Millennial Expectations and Jewish Liberties: A Study of the Efforts to Convert the Jews in Britain, up to the Mid Nineteenth Century* (Leiden, 1978), 91,129.

26. Editorial, *Florida Herald and Southern Democrat (St. Augustine)*, 3 December 1841.

27. James M. Denham, *"A Rogue's Paradise," Crime and Punishment in Antebellum Florida, 1821-1861* (Tuscaloosa and London, 1997), 226-82.

28. It has been long held that Levy's father, Eliahu Levy, was vizier or prime minister. First-hand accounts contradict this belief. See Norman A. Stillman and Yedida K. Stillman, "The Jewish Courtier Class in Late Eighteenth-Century Morocco as Seen Through the Eyes of Samuel Romanelli," in *Essays in Honor of Bernard Lewis: The Islamic World From Classical to Modern Times* (Princeton, 1989), 845-51; William Lempriere, *A Tour from Gibraltar to Tangier, Sallee, Mogodore, Santa Cruz, and Tarudant; and thence over Mount Atlas to Morocco, including a particular account of the Royal Harem* (Philadelphia, 1794)174-5. Lempriere notes there were seven Jewish under-secretaries of the treasury. He also relates the horrific death of the vizier. For a contemporary description of Eliahu Levy, see Samuel Romanelli, *Travail in an Arab Land*, trans. Yedida K. and Norman A. Stillman (1792:

Introduction

Reprint, Tuscaloosa: University of Alabama Press, 1989).

29. M. E. Levy to Rachel [Levy] Henriques, 1 September 1853, Yulee Papers, PKY. Depression also surfaced after financial difficulties following the Seminole war. See "Notes of manuscript writings of M. E. Levy ", 24 October 1843 and February 1850, Yulee Papers, PKY. These "uncontrollable" episodes, combined with Levy's prodigious output of energy and drive, suggests the possibility of bi-polar disorder.

30. For Levy's account of this experience see M. E. Levy to Rachel [Levy] Henriques, 1 September 1853, Yulee Papers, PKY.

31. Ibid.

32. Contrary to most assumptions, Eliahu Levy actually died in Gibraltar. See *Florida Herald and Southern Democrat*, 24 February 1846. For a first-hand account of the plague (1799-1800) and its spread into Spain, see James Grey Jackson, *An Account of the Empire of Marocco* (London, 1814), 171-187. This epidemic is briefly noted in Joseph Toledano, *La Saga des Familles les Juifs du Maroc et Leurs Noms* (Tel Aviv, 1983), 232.

33. Leon Huhner, "Moses Elias Levy, Florida Pioneer," *Florida Historical Quarterly* 19 (April 1941): 320.

34. Adler, "Attempts to Colonize Florida", 19; Notorial Protocol for St. Thomas, Yulee Papers, PKY. Moses and Hannah Levy were married 16 March 1803. 1805 is the first year Levy is recorded as the head of household. Aside from his wife and son, 3 "full grown" slaves are listed. His wife's maiden name of Abendanone—or Abendanan—is also of Moroccan Jewish origin. See *Encyclopaedia Judaica*, 1st ed., s.v. "Abendanan."; Shlomo Deshen, *The Mellah Society: Jewish Community Life in Sherifian Morocco* (Chicago and London, 1989), 8.

35. Levy relates his lean financial years starting out in business in M. E. Levy to Rachel [Levy] Henriques, 1 September 1853, Yulee Papers, PKY.

36. Samuel Proctor, "Pioneer Jewish Settlement in Florida; 1765-1900," in *Proceedings of the Conference on the Writing of Regional History in the South with Special Emphasis on Religious and Cultural Groups* (Miami Beach, 1956), 86; For confirmation of Philip and Judah P. Benjamin's relationship, see Isidor Paiewonsky, *Jewish Historical Development in the Virgin Islands, 1665-1959* (St. Thomas, 1959).

37. Levy's relationship with the Ramírez family is laid out in fascinating detail in M. E. Levy, letter to the editor, *Florida Herald and Southern Democrat (St. Augustine)*, 1 February 1843 and 23 January 1843. Also see René Veláquez, "The Intendancy of Alejandro Ramírez in Puerto Rico—1813-

Introduction

1816," (Ph.D. diss., University of Michigan, 1972), 32.

38. Notorial Protocol for St. Thomas 1815-16, Yulee Papers, PKY:"We have lived in discord for several years, led a most painful life and even so far, that we in more than three years have found ourselves obliged to live entirely separated."

39. "Narrative of my administration of my father's estates–Relations with my father's family", Yulee Papers, PKY. After his father's death, David Levy Yulee broke the stipulations of his will and appointed himself administrator.

40. Circular Letter and Resolution of the Hebrew Society of New York, 9 May 1821, Myers Family papers, Manuscript Collection No. 480, Box 3, American Jewish Archives, Cincinnati, Ohio. See also Joseph Gary Adler, "Moses Elias Levy and Attempts to Colonize Florida," in *Jews of the South: Selected Essays from the Southern Jewish Historical Society*, ed. Samuel Proctor, Louis Schmier (Macon, GA., 1984), 22.

41. Ibid.

42. Ibid., 25, n.25.

43. Huhner, "Moses Elias Levy", 325-6, 329, 331.

44. For Levy's reference to actual Jewish settlers see M. E. Levy to Rachel [Levy] Henriques, 1 September 1853, Yulee Papers, PKY: "You undertake to tell me what I ought to have done–namely to establish 3 or 4 Jewish families on farms near me–this I tried to do, but it is not easy to transform old clothes men or stock brokers into practical farmers–this was the prospect which carried me to England in 1824 . . . ." This, in addition to Frederick Warburg's presence at Pilgrimage, contradicts Adler's assertion that "it is most unlikely" any Jews came to his settlement.

Levy's plantation was located about two and one-half miles west of the present town of Micanopy between Ledwith and Levy Lakes. Caroline Barr Watkins, *The Story of Historic Micanopy* (Gainesville, FL, 1976), 29.

Micanopy was named for the hereditary Seminole chief of the area; the town was known by that name from its beginnings in 1821. See *East Florida Gazette* (Saint Augustine), 23 July 1821.

45. M. E. Levy to Reuben Charles, 12 August 1824, Meta Shaw Coleman Collection, PKY. For Warburg's genealogy, see *Stam- und Nachfahrentafein der Familie Warburg* (Hamburg, 1937), 37. For Warburg's participation in the operation of Levy's plantation, see F. Warburg, "List of Articles delivered to me on the Pilgrimage Plantation which is under my charge," [n.d.], Meta Shaw Coleman collection, PKY. See also, Adler, "Attempts to Colonize Florida," n.9.

Introduction

46. M. E. Levy to [Jonathan] Dacosta, 18 September 1845, Yulee Papers, PKY: "Having expended all my ready means I was obliged to go to Europe to forward my views." (Levy previously visited England in 1816 while still engaged as a merchant in the West Indies.)

47. Toledano, *Juifs du Maroc*, 232. The Levy Ben Yuli (Ha-Levi Ibn Yuli) family had a long history as merchants to the Sultans of Morocco.

48. Toury, "M. E. Levy's Plan," 23.

49. M. E. Levy to Isaac L. Goldsmid, 25 November 1825, in Toury, "M. E. Levy's Plan," 29.

50. Huhner, "Moses Elias Levy," 338.

51. *The World* (London), 4 June 1828. Levy's connections with the Philo-Judeans is reviewed in Toury.

52. "Extract of a letter from a clergyman from Bristol," *The World* (London), 9 January 1828.

53. Levy placed ads in German Jewish newspapers soliciting settlers to come to Florida as late as November 1825. See, Huhner, "Moses Elias Levy, Florida Pioneer", 331.

54. Todd M. Endelman, *The Jews of Georgian England, 1714-1830: Tradition and Change in a Liberal Society* (Philadelphia, 1979), 71-73; Scult, *Millennial Expectations*, 104-5.

55. Endelman, *Jews of Georgian England*, 132-36.

56. "Notes of manuscript writings of M. E. Levy", Yulee Papers, PKY, 81: "The Bible is true and the teachers are false."

57. Endelman, *Jews of Georgian England*, 163; Adler, "Moses Elias Levy," 20. For Levy's views toward Orthodox Judaism, see Forster and Levy, *Present Condition of the Jews*, 7: "I differ essentially both with Christians and Jews in general, on this point, viz. that doctrines respecting essentials should not be deduced from any system founded on mere comments on the Word of God; for a doctrine of faith, however apparently mysterious, should be, in my opinion, unequivocally revealed . . ."

58. Howard R. Greenstein, *Turning Point: Zionism and Reform Judaism* (Chico, CA., 1981), introduction.

59. M. E. Levy, "Speech addressed to a meeting of Jews and Christians," *The World* (London), 28 May 1828. Levy expounds in detail on a utopian vision of a Divinely inspired Israel: "The poor and the rich, the master and the slave, and even the stranger, sympathizing in the same feelings and banishing all distinctions, regarded each other as members of the same family."

Introduction

60. Howard Temperley, "Anti-Slavery as Cultural Imperialism," in *Anti-Slavery, Religion and Reform: Essays in Memory of Roger Anstey*, ed. Christine Bolt and Seymour Drescher (Folkestone, Eng., 1980), 338.

61. Forster and Levy, *Present Condition of the Jews*, vi. "Mr. Levy . . . made his name so well known as to render any further introduction of him to public notice unnecessary."

62. M. E. Levy, "Speech addressed to the 2nd Meeting of the Catholic Mission," *The World* (London), 18 June 1828. Levy addresses the topic: "Is Slavery Compatible with the Principals of Revelation?"

63. Thomas Thrush, *Letters to the Jews: Particularly Addressed to Mr. Levy of Florida* (York, 1829), 99. Thrush was affiliated with the London Society and dedicates the book to the membership. The London Society was more aggressive in its conversion tactics than its offshoot, the Philo-Judeans. See Endelman, *Jews of Georgian England*, 71-73.

64. Quoted in *The World* (London), 20 August 1828.

65. James Walvin, *Slavery and British Society 1776-1846* (Baton Rouge, 1982), 15.

66. [M. E. Levy], *A Plan for the Abolition of Slavery, Consistently with the Interests of all Parties Concerned* (London, 1828), 29.

67. M. E. Levy, "Speech addressed to the 2nd Meeting of the Catholic Mission," *The World* (London), 18 June 1828.

68. [Levy], *Abolition of Slavery*, 13.

69. Thomas D. Hamm, *God's Government Begun: The Society for Universal Inquiry and Reform, 1842-1846* (Bloomington, 1995), xvii. "Immediatism" was also beginning to be dominant among Quaker abolitionists in the Northern U.S. during this time, and the very act of slaveholding was itself considered a sin.

70. [Levy], *Abolition of Slavery*, 18.

71. *The World* (London), September 1828.

72. Ibid.

73. [Levy], *Abolition of Slavery*, 29.

74. Quoted in Toury, "M. E. Levy's Plan," 27.

75. M. E. Levy to John Forster, [n. d.] 1828, in Forster and Levy, *Present Condition of the Jews*, 17.

76. Quoted in Toury, "M. E. Levy's Plan", 27.

77. M. E. Levy, letter to the editor, *Florida Herald and Southern Democrat (St. Augustine)*, 11 January 1843.

78. [Levy], *Abolition of Slavery*, 13.

Introduction

79. Temperley, "Anti-Slavery as Cultural Imperialism", 347.

80. *Florida Herald and Southern Democrat (St. Augustine)*, 3 December 1841. These remarks were written in an editorial under the heading "The Case of David Levy".

81. [Levy], *Abolition of Slavery*, 15-7.

82. Ibid., 15.

83. Ibid., 16.

84. Ibid.

85. Ibid., 11.

86. M. E. Levy to John Forster, 2 May 1828, in Forster and Levy, *Present Condition of the Jews*, 50.

87. Ibid., M. E. Levy to John Forster, 28 August 1828, 82.

88. Samuel Proctor, "Pioneer Jewish Settlement," 89.

89. Ibid., 91. Samuel Proctor considers Levy's *Letters Concerning the Present Condtion of the Jews* (1829), as the first such publication. Levy's pamphlet preceeds this by one year.

90. Korn, *Jews and Negro Slavery*, 13.

91. [Levy], *Abolition of Slavery*, 12.

92. Korn, *Jews and Negro Slavery*, 66

93. M. E. Levy to Rachel [Levy] Henriques, 1 September 1853, Yulee papers, PKY; *The Floridian (Tallahassee)*, 23 January 1836.

94. M. E. Levy to Rachel [Levy] Henriques, 1 September 1853, Yulee papers, PKY.

95. Ibid.

96. Ibid.

97. M. E. Levy disinherited both his sons (giving each $100) in his will dated 1838. He intended his estate to be divided among his two daughters and his sister, but his son David broke these stipulations and shared in the inheritance. See "Last Will and Testament", Levy File, St. Augustine Historical Society, St. Augustine, Florida; David Yulee, "Narrative of my administration of my father's estates," Yulee Papers, PKY.

98. [Levy], *Abolition of Slavery*, 3.

99. Proctor, "Pioneer Jewish Settlement," 91.

100. Quoted in Huhner, "Moses Elias Levy, Florida Pioneer", 336.

Micanopy, Florida   CHRIS MONACO
October 22, 1999

A

PLAN

FOR THE

Abolition of Slavery,

CONSISTENTLY

WITH   THE   INTERESTS

OF

ALL   PARTIES   CONCERNED.

LONDON:

PUBLISHED BY GEORGE SIDFORD,

25, LUDGATE-HILL;

AND SOLD BY ALL BOOKSELLERS.

PRICE EIGHT-PENCE.

1828.

TO

THE RELIGIOUS PUBLIC

THIS   PAMPHLET

IS

RESPECTFULLY

AND

AFFECTIONATELY DEDICATED

BY THE AUTHOR

London, July 1st, 1828

A PLAN

FOR THE

ABOLITION OF SLAVERY,

&c.

HAVING devoted my attention to the abolition of Slavery for the last twenty years, under peculiarly advantageous circumstances, I feel anxious to contribute my mite to the general stock of information on this interesting subject, that those who are manfully labouring to effect this great object may be in possession of all information likely to throw light on the subject. I have resided in slave-holding countries for more than twenty-four years, and, during that time, I have experienced the weaknesses and infirmities, the temptations and passions, which are incident to slave-owners. The lessons which this state of things necessarily conveys to reflective minds, led to the inquiry as to the best mode of counteracting its effects, at least, in my own family.

But, the more I examined the subject, the more complicated it appeared to me; and often did I, in a tone of despair, pronounce the case hopeless. This may easily be conceived, when it is said, that, in tracing effects to causes, we find that the present vices of the slave are but the effects of those of the owner; and that those of the owner are likewise the effects resulting from those of the slave; and that, consequently, the moral degradation of both renders *any reform originating in themselves, impracticable.* The severe measures adopted by the master seem called for by the vices of the slave; and these, again, are requisite, to pamper the weaknesses and passions of the avaricious master. Such insurmountable obstacles might have put a stop to my endeavours; did not their effect manifestly operate on my children, already labouring under many moral incapacities, originating from another, and a more inveterate, source:

and thus, in reflecting on the one, the other, as it were, sympathetically presented itself; until, from motives of principle, the one became identified with the other. This train of reflection ultimately led me to the knowledge of one great truth,—that, as Providence works to effect a certain end for the benefit of all mankind, no man must be operated upon by the same spirit in all his actions; and that, consequently, it is impossible to attempt to injure or benefit any part of the family of man without operating, either directly or indirectly, on the whole. When, therefore, man loses sight of this great truth, however good his intention or action may be, if confined to any single community in its operation, he will inevitably encounter conflicting interests, and meet with obstacles to impede its progress. This view, in my opinion, answers the questions put by Mr. Denman, in his admirable speech at the last anniversary meeting of the Anti-Slavery Society.—"Why have we made so little progress in the great cause of emancipation? Why have the colonists evaded the resolutions submitted to them by the mother country for these five years?" It is, I say, because the *true* interests of both slave and owner, not only with respect to this, but to ALL other slave-holding states, are not unitedly consulted and manfully attacked. The question in the abstract, and the relation it bears to the civilized and religious world, is so momentous, that, without a thorough acquaintance with its extent and importance, it will be impossible to ascertain the degree of evil arising from a system of slavery, the ruinous consequences it threatens, or the nature of the remedy which might be successfully applied. The European reader must, however, be impressed with this fact, that *the black and white inhabitants of the colonies cannot possibly be expected to sympathise or unite, at least for some time, in civil or domestic intercourse.* The eastern and some of the middle states of America afford a good example of this fact; nay, I will even instance the Society of Friends in that country; that class of individuals have ever displayed indefatigable zeal in the cause of emancipation; they will make any effort to promote this their darling object; yet have we no instance of their taking a genteel coloured family or person by the hand of unqualified friendship, intermarrying with them, or even mixing in social or convivial pleasure. This fact the philosopher and legislator should not lose sight of, in their speculations on this most delicate question. Whether the prejudice will be undermined by some stronger motive, I will not, at present, venture to assert; but, as far as mere reasoning goes, this great barrier will not be easily removed by mere human effort; and he who would legislate without considering the consequences to which this prejudice may give rise, in a mixed community governed by laws of equal rights, can possess but a limited degree of knowledge of the human heart. Is it not natural, I would ask, that minds operated upon by innate and insurmountable prejudices should produce correspondent resentment and ill-will in the heart of frail man, whether white or black? What will be the consequence of placing the injured and resentful untaught negro on a level, in civil rights, with the haughty and imperious civilized white? Will nine or ten hardy blacks submit to the contemptuous and haughty treatment of one of their white fellow citizens; when, in addition to the confidence which numbers and physical strength must necessarily inspire them with, the laws afford them but the power of revenging themselves on their oppressors by stratagem, cunning, or perjury? Let us suppose, that the slaves in the British colonies are emancipated by Act of Parliament:—will the feeling of gratitude be sufficient to make them overlook the personal as well as mental advantages of the whites, who are constantly reflecting on their inferiority? Let us allow, for a moment, that the limited number of enervated whites in the British colonies will, by some unknown effort of the mind, be led to act so as to make their black fellow-subjects feel their inferiority as little as possible:—will the untutored negro be blind to the degradation in which his race is held all over the other parts of the world? Will mere motives of gratitude teach him to distinguish between the white skin of an Englishman and that of other white oppressors? Let him who would for a moment entertain such a theory look at St. Domingo. Were the slaves not made free and equal citizens, in one single day, with their masters? Did gratitude prevent the massacre of all the white inhabitants of the island? The charity of Englishmen may give freedom to the slaves of their own colonies; but it will avail nothing, as against the general feeling entertained towards this unhappy race all over the world. Will their charity mould their own nature, to view with equal complaisance the symmetrical form and the fair skin of an European, and the disproportioned figure and black skin of an African? the long auburn tresses, and the woolly hair? the well-shaped and polished forehead, and a depressed one? the finely-shaped nose, and the short, flat, wide nose? the cherry lips of an European, and the thick black ones of an African? It is within the power of legislation or money to emancipate 800,000 slaves; but is there any legislative act, *except that of God*, that can counteract such insurmountable prejudices? I will even go further, and, laying aside the question of emancipation, suppose the present slaves qualified to appear as witnesses in courts of justice, not only the property, life, and honour of the master are exposed, but eventually the whites will become the slaves of the blacks. Be it so, it may be said. But, if the government be once in the hands of the blacks, will the colonies remain for any time under the British dominion? Let the colonies go,—I may be answered. But, then, will such a state of things benefit the blacks? Will any vessel be able to navigate those seas strewed with innumerable small islands, inhabited by a small number of people of unequal power, and, consequently, of conflicting interests? But what alternative have we? Shall we, it may be asked, to avoid such evils, continue the unjust system of slavery? No: not only justice, but policy, forbids it: for, by continuing it, you necessarily produce a worse state of things,—a state in which the whole religious and civilized world is materially concerned,—a state which threatens the earth with a scourge, to retaliate on and punish the oppressors of the unhappy sons of Africa, enslaved for nearly three centuries.

It is to this awful side of the picture that I solicit the reader's most particular attention. Let us, for the present, view the question but in a political light. The prospect which opens upon Europe and America, if some timely steps be not resorted to, is neither more nor less than that of anarchy, and all its demoralising effects, for centuries to come, which will ultimately end in the establishment of the dominion of the blacks; and that rich portion of the American territory, extending from Chesapeake Bay, in the United States, to Rio de la Plata, in South America, will become another New Guinea. By the census of 1810, in the United States, the black population amounted to nearly two millions of souls. Their increase is very rapid: and, although the population there is as four whites to one black, yet this proportion is only found in classing the northern, middle, and southern States together; for, if we limit ourselves to the southern States, the proportion will be found in favour of the blacks.

Let us now throw a prospective glance on this state of things, fifty or one hundred years hence, when the present number of blacks will have increased to eight or even to sixteen millions. Can such a number exist, in a rich and extensive territory, reaching from the Atlantic to the Pacific, without becoming formidable? Yet, formidable as such a power is in itself, it will even become greater, by the moral strength they must necessarily receive from the Island of Cuba, whose black population must now amount to nearly the whole number of slaves in the British colonies. This large island, nearly 700 miles long, cannot but shortly follow the example of its neighbouring power, St. Domingo; as must, likewise, Jamaica. What mighty empires each of these islands is capable of forming, to the annoyance of posterity, and united by the strongest of ties, *the unconquerable hatred and prejudice of the whites!* Pursuing, in our course, the line of islands and keys which are thickly scattered in that part of the ocean, and which must prove more dangerous to the peace and tranquillity of nations, from their insignificant size, we arrive at that unhealthy coast of the Guianas. As the climate of this extensive territory of low-lands has ever proved more destructive to the enervated whites, under their hitherto slave-driving system, than any other country, no increase in the already insignificant and disproportionate white population can be expected; while the coloured people, who, from their rural and laborious employments, accommodate their nature to the climate, must increase in a surprising degree.

We now come to the vast empire of the Brazils. Here we must pause, and attentively contemplate the situation and policy of this southern extreme of the future New Guinea. The population of this fertile and extensive territory consists, like the rest, of a greater number of blacks than whites. The slave trade is still carried on to an alarming extent, and, from its contiguity to Africa, it would be impossible, without extraordinary vigilance, to suppress it. From the great facilities afforded by the numerous unfrequented harbours, bays, and creeks, a Brazilian planter might, without much risk of detection, sail with a vessel and cargo of the value of from 500*l.* to 1000*l.* to the opposite coast, and return with a supply of 100 or 200 negroes for his plantation. Now what can be the result, but that, in process of time, that great extent of free America will be converted into a species of New Guinea. We here behold this skeleton of a future gigantic power, in as formidable a position as a well-adapted combination of circumstances can make it; North America on the one hand, and the Brazils on the other; while, in the centre, is the chain of islands on one side, and Guiana, Venezuela, and central America on the other; whose population, at present, according to the most moderate calculation, is at the ratio of seven coloured persons to one white. What renders this picture still more gloomy is, that the newly-formed States in that part of the world are feeble, from the unwieldy extent of territory occupied by their thinly scattered population. The many evils resulting from this circumstance, combined with the inveterate vices inherited from the parent nations, must render the protection of the lives and properties of the settlers extremely precarious: hence emigration from Europe cannot be expected to keep pace with the increase of coloured population. Will, then, the present degraded and debased slaves, when they shall have arrived at that ascendancy with which their growing numbers must one day invest them, possess a due sense of justice, morality, or religion, to temper the savage ferocity natural to injured and frail man in a straggling, extensive territory? I will leave it to the contemplative mind to form a true picture of the state of such countries a century hence, if not counteracted by timely, wise, and active measures. *Will not the religious mind be apt to perceive, in such a state of things, the retributive hand of Justice preparing a scourge to chastise the whites for the oppression they have, for so many centuries, been guilty of towards* *the unfortunate sons of Africa?* It would, I fear, be useless to call on Spain or Portugal, as originators of the slave-trade, to redress the wrongs of the unhappy negroes: for they are already on the edge of the vortex which the sins of their forefathers have been preparing for them, and into which they seem even now to be hurrying. It is England, and her offspring on the other side of the Atlantic, France, and Holland—in fact, all the influential potentates of Europe, who should advance with united interest to warn the Brazilians of the impending danger which they, by speedy and wise measures, might be able to avert.

Before, however, we touch on the best means of averting this threatened evil, I will make a few observations on the obstacles which the internal interest of the different nations have to contend with, in addition to those which emancipation presents, morally and abstractedly speaking.

The raising of sugar, as hitherto pursued in the West Indies, is held to be impracticable by free labour. To this I am inclined to give full credence. To detail all that could be advanced in its support would swell this pamphlet to an inconvenient length. The principal reason appears to be this: that, as the cultivation of the cane, the manufacturing of the sugar, and the distilling of the rum, are all united in one concern; and, as each separately does not require the number of hands that are often necessary, on some urgent occasions, for a short time, the planter would be unable, without incurring great expense, to provide against the risk of losing unforeseen favourable moments, if the requisite number of labourers could not be promptly obtained. Slaves, therefore, whose time may be disposed of at command, seem to be necessary, both for the success of the undertaking, and for raising the commodity at a reasonable price. To convince those who are unacquainted with this species of occupation, I will merely refer to St. Domingo. Their principal staple, while the soil was worked by slaves, was sugar; whereas, now, coffee has taken its place: nay, the Haytians, until lately, imported sugar for their own consumption. However feasible, therefore, the raising of sugar by free hands may appear to be, under a new system and a new colony, it could not possibly be enforced in establishments which have been carried on under a system of slavery for centuries past, without great loss of property and a complete change in the characteristic features of the different branches of industry, policy, morals, legislation, &c. This obstacle is justly felt by the proprietors and legislators of the West Indies, and very inconsiderately overlooked by European philanthropists and philosophers. Thus we see, that if the slaves are emancipated, we have to contend, first, against the legal claims of proprietors, not only with respect to the property which, by law, they have in the slave, but as proprietors of the soil and the extensive sugar manufactories, which must fall in value if the present system of agriculture be altered; secondly, it is a well-known fact, that the English proprietor is only concerned in the West India interest as far as pecuniary considerations go; for, his object is to acquire an independence, and retire to England; consequently, he could not be expected to make any willing sacrifice to secure the future prosperity of a community with whom he is not morally identified. Nothing but force could compel the colonists to legislate against their pecuniary interest; and, if even prevailed on to enact any laws in favour of the slave, they would be but a dead letter: for lawyers, witnesses, jurors, and magistrates, are all interested parties. Thirdly, the vices and ignorance of both masters and slaves. Fourthly, the prejudices of the white against the black, and the corresponding hatred it engenders in the breast of the black. Fifthly, the impossibility of counteracting this prejudice in any *single* community, while the degradation of the blacks is universal. And, sixthly, the want of consideration, on the part of the Europeans, in urging emancipation without contributing any other aid towards it than clamour, and in expecting that the slaves could be emancipated by the sole interference of government.

Thus we are surrounded by difficulties on all sides, and, in either case, civilized society is threatened with greater evils than those inflicted by the slave-dealers on the oppressed sons of Africa. If the impending mischief be not averted by timely measures, the Americans will entail on their future posterity more suffering than the slaves ever experienced from the galling chains and merciless whip of their forefathers. Before, however, I proceed to offer any remarks on the remedy which sixteen or eighteen years' deliberation has suggested to my mind, it is necessary to observe, that only those persons who both acknowledge *and feel* the influence of Divine Revelation (and not the mere philanthropist) are capable of undertaking the work proposed, or of effecting any good in the cause: for it must be granted, that the past sufferings and oppression of the blacks, however just with respect to the dispensation of Providence, are unjust on the part of those who have acted as oppressors for their own private interest. To avert, therefore, the retribution which justice demands, it is not only necessary to abandon the system of persecution and oppression hitherto pursued against the blacks, *but to turn that very system into an instrument of blessing to the uncivilized Africans.*

This language neither the mere philosopher nor the mere philanthropist can comprehend: it can only be felt by those who are operated upon by the principles of the revealed word of God. It is such, and such alone, who are capable of perceiving the impracticability of prevailing against the contending interests and prejudices in which the question is involved, unless the work be undertaken in the spirit of atonement for past aggressions, and in order to promote the purposes of God.

From the nature of the obstacles which lie in the way of emancipation, the remedies necessary to counteract them appear to me to be these:—First, that the proprietors should not be the only sufferers in the cause of emancipation, but that *every individual, both in Europe and America, should equally lend their aid in the cause:* for, were we to examine the question fairly, we should find that every one in Europe, as well as in America, has profited, either directly or indirectly, by the system of slavery, and has, consequently, assisted in oppressing its subjects. Secondly, that legislation for the amelioration of the condition of the slaves, should not be entrusted to slave owners. Thirdly, that the slaves, being naturally unaccustomed to think for themselves, and being habitually indolent, deceitful, and vicious, from the effects of their abject state, should be suffered to die as slaves, and even continue, with some gradual alterations, under the accustomed oppressive government in which they were born and bred. Fourthly, that a practical, substantial, and religious education should be given to the rising generation, both of the whites and blacks. Fifthly, that the system of agriculture, in general, should be altered, particularly with respect to raising sugar. Sixthly, that the emigration of white people should be encouraged. Seventhly, that some period should be fixed, when slavery shall cease in the whole continent of America and all the West Indian isles. And, lastly, that companies should be established in every civilized nation to co-operate in carrying these things into effect indiscriminately, *by example in all slave-holding countries.*

This last remedy is, in my opinion, so essential, that, without it, no reform could be really effected: for unless, as I previously observed, slavery could be attacked, in general, by a well-defined and plain universal system, existing prejudices cannot be so effectually overcome, as to render an equal participation in civil rights safe. By having chartered companies to carry on a system of agriculture agreed upon, or any other measure, in every place, the interests will be united, and the policy of the several governments will receive a check when it interferes with private interests; by which means, the system will be carried on under the stability and guarantee of unanimity.

The plan or system to be proposed, is as follows:—That chartered companies shall be established in Europe, and also in America, for the purpose of abolishing slavery in the civilized world, by means of education, and a new system of agriculture; and that they shall obtain, from the different governments interested in it, a concordat, declaring some specified period when slavery shall cease to exist,—say 50 or 100 years hence. My opinion is, that mankind generally fail in their projects, by endeavouring to sow and to reap before the proper time and season. The emancipation of the slaves should not be aimed at until they are rendered capable of enjoying and of deserving their freedom. If this be not first attended to, their liberty will prove as great a curse to them as the free institutions of this country, or the United States of America, would be to the Algerines or the Cannibals. Lord Melville proposed, in 1792, that the slaves shall be declared free in 1800. Had this statesman said in 1850, the friends of emancipation might have been nearer the attainment of their desires than they are at present. Indeed, 50 or 60 years are even too limited a period, unless great exertions are used, to prepare the slaves to receive the blessing of freedom; it is scarcely sufficient time to allow their owners to dispose of their property, or to direct their operations to an opposite system than the one under which they were established, or to train their children to different pursuits and habits than the usual ones.

If all the civilized powers were, with one consent, to fix the emancipation of the slaves at some reasonable period, the owners, perceiving themselves considerately dealt with, and that, if the slaves were not prepared for their freedom at a fixed period, they would obtain it by severe means, would not only acquiesce in the measure, but even be induced to co-operate and forward a cause that would ultimately redound to their own safety. From the mere fact, that emancipation is decided on at a stated period, by the united voices of the civilized powers of Europe, all unreasonable tongues will be silenced. The slaves, on their part, will direct their expectations to the same distant object and certain hope; which will put an end to that dangerous state of mind which deferred hope creates, arising from the circumstances of being aware that their masters resist granting a freedom which the Europeans are labouring to gain for them. Nay, the blacks will, by losing all hopes of freedom for themselves, and centring them in their offspring, learn a lesson that will operate to advantage on their moral character: viz., that *they* are *unfit* to be freemen, from possessing the vices of slaves, but that their rising generation will be made deserving of receiving that blessing.

It will be further the duty of the United Association zealously to inquire into and suggest to government the best and most effectual means of annihilating the slave-trading system: for, however inclined the separate governments may be to promote this object, yet, if they do not all *unite*, both in counsel and means, to destroy that inhuman traffic, in vain will be all the labour which they may individually bestow. It is of very little use for any single power to send agents to Spanish colonies or

Portuguese settlements, to prevent the introduction of any more slaves: for, were the agent to report any infraction of such orders in places where they are practised, his life would pay the forfeit; nay, he dares not even notice the prohibited Africans being landed before him. This I know from experience. It is, therefore, the slave-coast that must be guarded, not by England alone, but *by all nations*. Is there any nation more interested in guarding the coast than Brazil or Spain? I am aware that their subjects are, as yet, incapable of perceiving their own interest in its true light; but their governments might lead them to it. In fact, to employ an active vigilance on that coast is of the highest interest, not only to America, but to all Europe: for it is impossible to separate the interests of civilized society. It is, therefore, incumbent on all the American governments in particular, and on the European ones in general, to unite their efforts, in order to establish, by some equitable system of contribution, a formidable force or fleet of small vessels, under one head, at the different points of that continent, to be in an uninterrupted cruize against the slave traders.

It appears to me that such a plan might be adopted, at a very moderate expense, and would be the means of arresting the progress of that inhuman traffic which is the present source of the evil, but which, in ten years, if the proposed measures were followed up with energy, would be entirely forgotten.

To do this effectually, the management should be entrusted to one single nation. The vessels employed in such an enterprise should be of a peculiar construction, and fitted, in every respect, for the service; for those used by the slave traders are fast sailing, and calculated to beat to windward, upon which alone they depend on escaping from cruisers in tropical and calm latitudes. It appears to me, that if schooner-rigged vessels of about 150 to 200 tons were to be built at Bermuda, of light cedar-wood, and so constructed as to be navigated occasionally by steam, they might be of essential use in chasing a vessel upon the wind, or in a calm.* These steam-boats might be manned principally by natives, and commanded by able and expert men from the same place, or from the West India Islands. The expense of such a fleet would be less than the usual cost of those generally employed, and, at the same time, more real good would be effected. The Bermuda vessels are known to sail faster before or free from the wind than the sharp Baltimore schooners, and from the advantage of steam navigation they will possess a decided superiority over them upon the wind. Being manned by natives and persons inured

*The palm oil, which abounds on the coast of Africa, may be used with great advantage for fuel.

to the climate, the lives of many Europeans who now fall a sacrifice will be spared; and from the practice which a stationary employment will give to these men, they will prove more formidable than British officers and commanders, who must serve their apprenticeship at every change. Whilst such energetic measures are taken to prevent the further introduction of slaves into America, the united societies established in the different civilized countries must, on the other hand, direct their attention and labour to promote the emigration of white people to America—suggesting from time to time to the different governments the best means, which experience may teach them, to induce emigrants to settle in the infant states. This must evidently appear an object of the highest importance to the civilized world; for the emigration of white people to America will not only prove the most effectual method of destroying slavery, and of consolidating the newly-formed governments, but Europe itself will be greatly benefited. By this means she will be enabled to disencumber herself of her redundant population, and check the present alarming growth of crime, aggravated by the oppressing system of monopoly which the arts and sciences tend but to increase. Why is not the wise and humane measure adopted by England of transporting the greater part of her criminals to New South Wales, practised by all the other nations of Europe? Why do they not enter into some treaty with the new Governments of America to receive all those of their subjects whom want and misery have driven to vicious habits? The West Indies, Central America, Venezuela, Guiana, and Brazil, are all thinly populated—let them, therefore, receive the criminals of Europe as subjects; and if no other more humane means are as yet discovered to reclaim them, let them even be received as slaves. The spirit of the black population will be thus neutralized, and, by attending to the education of their freeborn offspring, the now wild wastes of America will be populated by an enlightened generation, in which the black skin will be lost with slavery in the gradual shades of improvement. Indeed, England herself might derive benefit by changing the present place of transportation to the West Indies or America. For the increase of crime is alarming, and the place of banishment is not longer a dread;—hence, far from deterring criminals, it, on the contrary, operates as an incentive to crime, for it procures them a free passage to a good country, where they may have a new field of action, and be screened from misery and want. A case which will illustrate the above statement was published in the *Times* newspaper a short time since. A number of privates belonging to a regiment which had been removed from New South Wales to Madras, actually committed felonies in order to return to their favourite country—preferring even to be sent thither in the degrading character of slaves or criminals to remaining in the luxuriant cantonments of the East Indies!* It could not be argued that policy requires the continuance of the present system of transportation to populate New South Wales, as the country possesses sufficient attractions to induce the choicest part of society to settle under its happy climate, without incurring the enormous expense which this country must be at, in transporting their criminals to so great a distance. If, instead of New South Wales, England were to substitute the West Indies, or South America, for her convicts, she would, while augmenting the population in those countries, increase her own interest and influence by spreading the enlightened habits and customs of her people, and necessarily increasing, in a proportionate degree, the demand for her own manufactures. In addition to these considerations, crime will receive some check from the dread of transportation to a climate considered unhealthy, which, with the horrors of West India slavery, will operate more powerfully on the mind than even the fear of death. If those criminals of Spain and Portugal who are condemned to the galleys were to be transported for life to Cuba, Porto Rico, or the Brazils, their condition might then be really ameliorated both in a temporal and a moral point of view. For what, in fact, is the miserable condition of a galley-slave?— It does not require any argument to convince those who are acquainted with the wretched state of these criminals, that death itself would be an improvement on a law said to be instituted from motives of humanity. As for France and Italy, they will find a sufficient field in their Palais Royales, their Galères, their Realtos, Bravos, Lazarones, &c. to furnish their quota of subjects; and they would thereby ease the coffers of the state, and remove a class of people from scenes which chain them to their vicious habits. In short, the benefit that would ensue from adopting such a course would be generally felt throughout Europe as well as America. It may be said that the criminals will contaminate the present inhabitants of the countries to which they may be transported. So they may, if left to themselves. I am aware that difficulties will attend the plan suggested for the first few years; but what are they when compared to the evils which a perseverence in the old system threatens to posterity? The planter will, perhaps, consult his private interest, and object to the introduction of intelligent subjects to act in a menial capacity, and who may be likely to disturb that debased state of mind necessary to make the slaves content to live on dried plaintains, and work six days in the week, to procure luxuries for a single individual. But it is

---

* Another case as late as last week was brought before a sitting magistrate, where the culprit candidly confessed that he stole a parcel of eleven pair of stockings in the hope of being transported, in order to save himself from misery and want. See the *Herald* newspaper of the 11th June, 1828.

now time that the selfish slave owner should be roused from his lethargy. It is time that he should be made to feel, if he cannot understand, that if he be not willing to lend his head and heart to promote the general good, the right of property which he claims in the slave is held but by a feeble tenure—that it is in reality but of a secondary consideration in the scale of the improvement of society—that if he look up to the community for the protection of his property, he must, on his part, contribute to the safety of that community. Were the subject, however, to be viewed in its true light, we should find that the planter would merely be required to sacrifice a little feeling in the change proposed. Let him but call forth the energies of a man, and he will be armed against all imaginary, as well as real, dangers. The change will not be as sudden and as formidable as he at a first glance may be led to fancy.

The criminal subjects which Europe might furnish cannot exceed fifty or sixty thousand souls; and the evils which might be anticipated from their depraved minds might be averted by the influence of those good and industrious persons which the tide of emigration would direct to that quarter. But even were this not to be the case, such a number is very insignificant when we consider the vast extent of territory and diversity of climate on the one hand, and on the other, the numerous useful occupations and trades in which they might be advantageously employed. The change at first would be scarcely felt before the system is tolerated, and the mind accommodated to the new state of things. I will, however, grant that the major part of the West India Islands, from their limited resources and their present system of agriculture, will not allow any great scope for emigration. But the large islands, such as Cuba, Jamaica, and Porto Rico, will most assuredly be able to receive subjects from Europe, who, although they may not intermingle with the negroes of established plantations, may nevertheless be employed in separate establishments of cotton, coffee, rum, &c. as also in different trades. It is true that the climate is an enemy to intemperate strangers, but this is one of the risks to which the laws of his country expose the criminal. The scheme is well worth a trial in Jamaica, Honduras, and Demerara; with respect to Cuba and Porto Rico, I am confident it will succeed, for the distance between the whites and blacks in Spanish countries is not so great as with the grave calculating Dutchman—the aristocratic Frenchman—or the high-minded, but haughty, Englishman. Often have I seen in Cuba, and Porto Rico, a white man working by the side of his slave and sitting at the same table. It appears to me that one reason why we find the Spanish creoles more identified with their native place, is because they are brought up to agricultural employments which serves their constitution and moulds their nature to the climate. Even the inundated country of the Choco contradicts the general assertion that the white people could not endure hard labour in tropical climates. The wagoners in Cuba are all white men, and the cultivators of tobacco, and graziers, are likewise generally of that class. It is owing to the circumstance that we do not perceive in Spanish colonies that disproportion in numbers between the whites and blacks as is invariably the case in other colonies. The population of these two islands, in 1815 and 1817, was at the rate of four white to five coloured persons in Cuba, and one white to two coloured in Porto Rico. Among the coloured population of these islands, there are many nearly white, who possess a competent and even affluent independence—nay, there are many families of the first respectability and influence in Cuba whose grandfathers or grandmothers were coloured persons. Their number, it is true, is comparatively limited, but this fact argues that the plan suggested in Spanish colonies is practicable. The reader will easily perceive that I have laboured to impress on his mind the necessity and practicability of European emigration to America and the West Indies; it is not, however, so much to the European that I address myself on this subject as to the creole. I know the difficulty attending a system which is likely to lower that idea of superiority which the planter deems so necessary for the negro to entertain towards a white person, however culpable or mean he may be. I know that the intelligence and vices of a white criminal may tend to counteract, not the purity of the negro's morals, but that stupid simplicity and abject submission to the white which transform the vices of the slave to virtues of the highest importance, which, although as pernicious to his soul as the most heinous crimes, yet are they deemed virtues, because they contribute to the replenishment of the master's purse.

I am aware that the plan suggested will be pronounced as monstrous by the white creole—but, at the same time, I know that it is his mistaken interest that blinds him and prevents him from understanding. I know that the West Indian nabobs will at first exclaim, and raise a clamour against the system, and endeavour by the best means in their power to counteract it, until they are convinced from experience that in raising the slave to the level of the white, although a criminal, and in debasing the white criminal to the level of the slave, they will both be benefited and attain to a higher state of excellence than the master can possibly conceive,—and he will one day feel happy to find himself on a level with the penitent slave, either white or black. Being thus aware of the difficulties which the slave owners will throw in the way of the proposed system, I am conscious that its introduction cannot be expected to originate with them; it must be done by the European societies, who are influenced by far higher motives than mere pecuniary interest. In short, let religion and piety be the sole guides and primary objects of such establishments, and the white criminal and vicious slave will breathe an atmosphere uncontaminated by the vices of either. But methinks I hear the creole, with all those angry feelings which some of them betray on such subjects, demand—" Do you then advocate indiscriminate marriages?" To this I reply—that if religion be not capable of allowing a connexion which mere animal passion gives rise to in slave-holding countries, we must then abandon the subject as hopeless, and consider the world to be governed by chance, there being two classes of beings, created with a prejudice against each other without the means of overcoming it. We can only then say—let America and the West Indies become another new Guinea, which, with the old one, shall unite to persecute the white people because they are not black, in the same manner as the white persecute the black because they are not white; and let brutal and indiscriminate passion effect what religion cannot.

The next object to which the societies should turn their attention, is that of promoting religious information, both amongst the whites and the blacks. As a preliminary, however, marriages, particularly amongst the blacks, should be encouraged; nay, even enforced by law; for how can we expect that religion or civilization shall find its way among persons compelled to live as brutes? Did the planter ever consult his interest— his pecuniary interest, he would enforce marriage amongst his slaves; for, surely, conjugal affection, parental and filial love, are the best guarantees for the good conduct of the subject. The planters of the Island of Cuba soon discovered the benefit of introducing marriage amongst the slaves. This reform was effected by so trivial an occurrence, and spread so rapidly, that I cannot but relate it. In the year 1812 or 13, a gentleman on a visit at a house of the most opulent planter in Havannah, Don P— de-la C— M—, met there, by chance, several planters of the highest rank— the subject of the moral condition of the blacks was discussed in the course of conversation. Some gave it as their opinion, that the mind of the black was incapable of cultivation, and that there was something naturally imperfect in its construction. The stranger remarked, that experience would contradict that position if the planter would apply the remedy which all savage nations did, to their great advantage, the blacks would yield to its influence as well as any other class of the sons of Adam. The remedy alluded to was the word of God — Religion! Oh! rejoined some of them; they are baptized, they confess once a year, &c. But how, replied the stranger, can confession be expected to avail if the sins are still persisted in? Are not the slaves by the most unjust discipline, obliged to live as brutes amongst themselves? Why not promote marriages amongst them. Try this, said he, and you will find it to be the best preparatory step to religious feelings; nay, added he, the very interest of the planter will benefit by such a system, for the affections of husbands, wives, parents, and children, will prove but so many ties to attach the slaves to their locations, and will make them more rational, more sober, and more useful inmates of the establishment. The conversation was put a stop to by a reply, that christians were far from doing their duty; and a pause ensued, which seemed to indicate that the argument had made some impression.

The stranger, two or three years after, revisited the Island of Cuba, and, to his astonishment, found the system of marriages spreading sympathetically on all the plantations in the Island. It appears that the above referred-to opulent planters, adopted the system of marrying the slaves on their own plantations, the salutary effect was soon felt and communicated to their neighbours, until it became a favourite discipline in all well-regulated plantations. Thus was a population of blacks, which must now be nearly 600,000, souls, by a mere hint, founded on the duties which the revealed word of God teaches, snatched from the brutalizing effects of a mistaken policy, which has, for so many generations, raged in the West Indian Isles. The change wrought in the condition of nearly 600,000 souls will be easily conceived, when the reader is told that, previous to this, the plantations had but a very inconsiderable number of females to the number of males.

I know of an instance, where an establishment of 1,000 negroes did not have fifty females amongst them.

I am aware, that it is impossible to enforce marriage in a plantation where the master would not be willing to facilitate it. But let a tax be imposed on all single persons in the colonies, and the planter will soon find it to his interest to promote legal marriages on his plantation.

This will be deemed a novel mode of legislating; be it so: if society require it, it is as fair a subject for legislation as any other.

I have attempted, hitherto, to point out the objects which the united societies should endeavour to promote. But, it is necessary to create a field of action, which, while it may prove the means of carrying their measures into effect, will tend to unite their interests and afford an opportunity to acquire experience; the only school which could promise success in so gigantic an undertaking. The plan proposed, is, in itself, simple, and such as money-making companies are even now pursuing. The object is to form agricultural establishments in those tropical countries, on a system adapted to free labour, the result of which will furnish the best argument to the planter, to induce him to change the present system for one which promises better returns. Such establishments might be undertaken by the different companies, individually or unitedly, with great advantage. In addition to the great end of abolishing slavery, destroying prejudice, and effectually improving the condition of millions of unborn souls, they would reap a good interest for their capital.* But ere I proceed, it will be necessary to lay before the reader the capabilities of lands in a tropical latitude; he will then be enabled to judge of the population which those regions are calculated to maintain, and, consequently, of the system of education, and proportionate ratio of cultivated minds, which the communities will require, in order to keep the intellect from becoming stagnant, as well as to counteract those evils, which laziness, an evil natural to warm climates and plenty, produces on the human mind.

A quarter of an acre of the banana tree will yield sufficient for the principal food of a family of ten persons; one quarter of an acre will produce from forty to fifty bushels of sweet potatoes; half an acre will give between twenty and forty bushels of maize and pease; and twenty

---

* English Capitalists, have, it is said, lent nearly seventeen millions sterling to the new states, which sickly and enfeebled Spain gave birth to, as weak in power as they are mighty in territories. For what purpose, I ask, were the loans made? Was it to secure or consolidate their freedom? No, far from it, for instead of benefiting the republics, they have done them much injury. Were the new governments actuated by true wisdom, they would have allowed their citizens to continue struggling with that poverty, and its attendant virtue, to which they owed their emancipation. The loans tended but to undermine that union, so essentially necessary to infant states (which a dependence on their own internal resources cements,) and to revive that cupidity, intrigue, and love of offices, so natural to the nation whence they sprang. These speculations may be deemed foreign to our subject, but they, nevertheless, impress the mind with this fact—that the burthen of debts incurred, cannot but add to the difficulties of the states, and augment their embarrassments, which must inevitably impede the growth of improvement. At the same time, it will call the attention of the stock-holders to the plan proposed, who will find their interest greatly connected with its success. While, from the present state of things, they are sensible of the little probability there is of receiving a dividend on the money already invested, they might, by uniting their interests, obtain from the governments of those extensive countries lands in lieu of interest. They might then employ their capital to much better advantage than in mining-bubbles, by establishing colonies on the plan proposed. The lands thus employed, will not only yield a sure and handsome return, but by the increase of an industrious population, contribute to bring the resources of the country into full operation, upon which alone the chance of the ultimate reimbursement of the original capital principally depends. Thus will a sum of money, now lying useless and inactive, be made, by judicious management, productive of much good, and be the means of diffusing happiness to hundreds of thousands, and, at the same time, accelerate the prosperity of a country, destined for the habitation of millions and millions of souls.

trees of coffee, if allowed to grow high, will give from two to three quintals yearly. Upon such a limited spot as one acre of land, a family of ten persons may actually raise provisions in a greater variety, and partake of more luxuries, than the plantation negro now enjoys; for the whole that he is allowed at present per week, is a peck of corn or a quota of plantains and a few herrings. If the family be enabled to add another acre of land, they may plant a quarter of an acre of sugar-cane, and raise sufficient small stock, such as fowls, pigeons, rabbits, and pigs, as to permit them to have animal food some part of the week. During the remainder, with their pepper-pot, pigeon-pease, cucumber, tania, and yarm soup, which may be seasoned with the †bene plant; their boiled corn flour, roasted or fried plantains, or potatoes, the family may have a good dinner, and thank their Maker for luxuries, of which many of their fellow creatures are deprived. As for their clothing, the present cost of each negro does not exceed 3*l.* per annum, which sum, with economy, will amply provide them with clothes suited to a warm climate. But this item will entirely depend on the industry of the family, who will provide themselves with clothing according to their circumstances, either by spinning, weaving, or other work. If, however, the plantation consist of four or five acres, they may have very decent clothing, as also pasture ground, to maintain a horse and cow, raise a few sheep or goats, and augment the variety of animal food, as well as other comforts. Thus it will be seen, that, with a plantation of five acres, a family of ten persons will live in a degree of comfort, provided their exertions be seconded by industry and religious habits, which a *consistent* system of education is alone capable of inculcating. And I will venture to assert that, provided this object be principally attended to, a farm of ten acres would enable them to move in a degree of refinement, and ensure to them more temporal comforts, than generally falls to the lot of the middling classes of farmers inhabiting those countries in Europe, which boast of a population of 200 souls to a square mile. But the reader will be apt to ask, why has this state of things never as yet been realized in tropical climates? The reason is clear; such a state is incompatible with a system of slavery, and the vices to which tyranny and an abject debased spirit give rise. It can only be realized in a state of freedom, when equal laws *and a substantial practical religious education* may be the patrimony of all classes of society, of the rich, as well as of the poor; it can only be realized in territories whose dense population can ensure stability to the government, and energy to the laws, both of which are incompatible with a thinly

†The Bene seed is said to yield eighty pounds of oil to every hundred weight; and when fresh, is of the sweetest flavour imaginable.

scattered population in an extensive territory, whose laws are based on tyranny and slavery. What an immense population the vallies of Aragua, and many other territories in Venezuela, might render happy, if that government were concentrated within itself, instead of being united to the unwieldly territory of New Grenada; an union, which will oblige the short sighted Bolivar to accept a crown, which his people, distracted by intrigue, and division of interest, must, sooner or later, force on his reluctant brow. The fertility of rich lands in a tropical climate and the capability of maintaining a more dense population than any other country, cannot at first glance be seen, from the system of agriculture at present pursued by the great planters of the British, Dutch, French or Danish settlements, though an estimate may be formed from the Spanish creole settlements. The frugal Spaniard of Europe, transmits his frugal habits to his creole descendants. With the lassitude occasioned by climate, want of education, a field of action for the exercise of his higher faculties, and the abundance with which nature supplies him, he is naturally inclined to lead a lazy and indolent life. If you visit one of the settlements in the interior of Porto Rico, or any other Spanish colony, amongst the peasantry, or that class of individuals, generally known under the name of Guagiros, you will there see a true picture of the degradation of the noble nature of man, when plenty, or the attainment of temporal enjoyment, is made the aim of his existence. The principal furniture of the house is a water jar, calabashes or cocoa mugs, cooking utensils, and stoves; a few plates, some wooden benches round an immensely large wooden table, two or three cots folded up in a corner of the room, and hammocks hung up in every direction, in which the members of the family rock their lives away. From the roof, you will see suspended, several branches of plantain, jerked beef or pork, sausages, and the like, and cocoa-nuts, melons, and other tropical fruits strewed about the floor; go when you will, you will find the hammocks in motion, while cards are briskly moving at one corner of the table; one and all, men, women, and even children, with cigars in their mouths. This class of people seems to exist but for the pleasure of sleeping away their lives, in their beloved hammocks. If a plaintain be within reach, when hungry, they will prefer it to a dainty dish, rather than leave their hammocks. No consideration will induce them to move, unless compelled by necessity, or for the gratification of any of their characteristic passions; to play at cards, attend at a cock-pit, or go to mass. But when once he is roused to business, he appears to go about it with so much alacrity, that one will scarcely recognize in him the lazy hammock-ridden Guagiro. He, however, soon flags, and relapses into his accustomed apathy, spending whole days and weeks in a vegetating state of torpidity. If you inquire into the means which a family of Guagiros have for their subsistence, you will find that whether they possess a large or a small tract of land, it consists of a *plantanal* or plantain ground, which requires no further attendance after once planted, than to cut down the luxuriant shoots, and clear the ground once every year or two; you will next find a few coffee trees for the use of the family, a small patch of sugar canes, all of which cost little or no trouble to raise. Sometimes they will have a small patch of potatoes or yams, which, with a few fruit trees, a horse, a cow, and a pig, completes the paradise of a Guagiro. Café con leche, coffee, with milk; cream-cheese crumbled in it; and roasted green plaintains, is their favourite breakfast and ready meal. Some will indulge in an ollia or soup at mid-day, while others will content themselves with a piece of broiled tasajo, jerked beef or pork, with boiled or roasted plantains, yams or potatoes. The supper is again café con leche, and the day closes but to usher in another of the same moral inanity.

We thus see that plenty, the palatable nature of the food, and the little trouble the grower has in procuring it, are the principal evils with which the inhabitants of tropical countries have to contend. Also that from such a state of ease, and in the absence of a dense population, regulated by a suitable government and cultivated minds, laziness must be the natural result, unless the system of slavery force man into action by the instrumentality of ambition, cupidity, and the luxuries and vices of a tyrant. M. de Humboldt goes further than I do in my calculations respecting the prolific produce of the plantain tree. He asserts that an acre of the plantain is capable of maintaining fifty persons, and hence it may be said to be one of the best gifts of the Author of nature for the support of man, as it is a plant which, without much labour, can be cultivated, reaped, and prepared, and forms a nutritious and agreeable food. The plantain, when green, furnishes a nutritious food, either roasted or boiled; when ripe, it possesses a sweet taste, rendered more delicious from an agreeable tinge of acid peculiar to the fruit. Whether it be boiled, roasted, or fried, it forms the best relish imaginable. There are many districts of white creoles amongst the Spaniards who live solely on this delicious and nutritive vegetable, without ever tasting bread. To give an idea of the nourishing properties of this plant, it will be sufficient to observe, that with all the laborious toils of the field, and the waste natural to the human frame in a warm climate, yet the greater part of the slaves live exclusively on it, without any other relish than a herring.

The sweet potato forms another nutritious plant. The yam likewise, when boiled or roasted, is used in lieu of bread. This is generally a favourite vegetable amongst the creoles, particularly if eaten with a salt relish. The cassava, which is obtained from the yuca, or manioc, forms another favourite diet. This farinaceous substance is, like the arrow root, obtained from the root of the plant. Of this flat cakes are made, or the flower is dried and may be preserved for use for years. By mixing it with boiling fish-water, or beef broth, seasoned with lime-juice and pepper, it makes a palatable food, and requires no other relish. The cake, as well as the flour soaked in water, is used, particularly amongst the French, in preference to bread. We next find the tania of different classes; its leaves make the finest spinach possible, and its root furnishes a more nutritious food than the Irish potato. In short, the tropical climate possesses so many vegetables which may be easily raised, and which are in their nature so agreeable to the palate, that unless the country be populated in proportion to its capabilities, and *under the influence of highly cultivated minds and a* RELIGIOUS SPIRIT, nothing can secure them from the trammels of slavery in its various shades, and the vices attendant on an easy and indolent life.

The position I take will be fully illustrated by referring the reader not to Africa but to the state of the inhabitants of the East and West Indies, as well as those of South America. The former having a dense population, with a portion of arts and sciences, but without the influence of Revelation; the latter with a thin population, consequently destitute of either art or science, possessing but a very imperfect idea of religion: both countries with tyrannic nabobs surfeited with luxuries earned by the hard labours of the multitude of poor rice or plaintain eaters. But if emancipation in America and the West India Islands be not allowed to cut a road for itself as chance may direct, but its steps beguile by the sure leading-strings of a consistent practical religious education; if the culti-vation of the soil be directed so as to bring the energies of the mind into healthful exercise, that it be kept from being surfeited by plenty, and impoverished by the apathy and laziness it creates, then the communi-ties, although small, may be formidable to others, and unitedly live happy and free within themselves. The arts and sciences will then keep pace with that degree of civilization which a closely united people is capable of, while a practical religious education will prevent civilization from de-generating into effeminacy, selfishness, cunning and deceit; a state which must be allowed to have ever proved the forerunner of injustice, corruption and slavery.

One objection, however, the philosopher may start against a high state of intellectual or moral attainment in a climate where the seasons are characterized with so great a degree of sameness as that experienced in tropical countries, where those marked changes from winter to summer are not felt, and hence the mind cannot experience those springs and falls to which it, in some measure, owes its energies. That warm climates are not inimical to the cultivation of science, the East Indies and ancient Egypt will fully prove. I will allow that the mind requires incentives, and a change in the field of action for the exercise and development of its precious powers. But if the imagination be kept from ranging in an extensive wilderness of plenty; if all the resources of the inventive mind be put in requisition by confining the population to the limits which the capabilities of the land, its local advantages, diversity of soil and productions, demand, agriculture will necessarily improve, and with it all branches of industry, and the comforts which such a state is calculated to produce will naturally create a sufficient field for the expansion and enlargement of the mind.

As I am addressing the religious, I am sure to be understood when I, in continuation, observe, that all the speculations of short-sighted philosophy will only prove true in that state of existence where the individual is moulded by education to act upon the principle that society, or the world, are objects of interest only so far as they contribute to his peculiar gratification. Then man may require different seasons to force his powers into action—then self-love, ambition, vain-glory, and the like, may prove as so many spurs to the development of some isolated power. But when a practical religious education shall bring the mind to a state far different to that of which mere morality is capable; when the mind is operated upon by those ever-varying and progressive stages of excellence which the word of God is alone capable of leading it into; when the word of God shall mould it to do the will of a creator who delights in the happiness of the individual, but as a part of the whole human family; then, instead of manifesting one or two isolated and detached powers which may be forced into action by the mere selfish bias of the individual, he will identify his happiness, and value it only as it contributes to that of the whole; which was, indeed, the aim and end of the creation. The noble mind, not confined by a selfish aim, but taking for its range the limits which the Creator has given for its end, will then unrestrainedly expand its powers; their degree of excellence being innate, and not tuitive.

Having expatiated upon the capabilities of tropical lands, and the influence they are calculated to produce on the character of the individual, and on society at large, and having previously argued the necessity of altering the present system of sugar establishments, I will now suggest to the united companies a plan which, if introduced with systematic perseverance, will, by the irresistible force of example, soon become general, and will show to the mistaken landed proprietors of those countries their true interest.

Let us suppose that a healthy location be chosen on both sides of a navigable stream, neasr to some populous town, and that, on its borders, a number of small plantations are located, of from two to ten acres of land each; that for every two or three hundred of these plantations there be established a sugar manufactory, the mill of which shall be worked either by the force of water, wind, or steam, which, when not employed in grinding the cane, may be used in sawing wood or grinding grain. Let each family, independent of their principal occupation or pursuit, grow from one to five acres of sugar-cane. When the season for grinding arrives, which is generally in the latter end of the fall, ten, twenty, or more families may, as neighbours, unite in cutting down the cane, and carrying them in boats to the manufactory. By paying the toll, which time and experience may fix, each shall be entitled to his portion of sugar which is to be assessed by competent judges amongst themselves, not with a saccharometer in the hand, but with the spirit of neighbourly consideration. On such an occasion, the best feelings will be excited. This festive season will be mutually hailed with joy. When the neighbours thus join with social and disinterested feelings, each will be prompted to vie with the other in showing kind and friendly assistance, and the sugar-making season may be rendered the means of cementing their family connexion. A faint picture of this may be imagined, if we figure to ourselves the description given us of the vintage season in wine countries. The planters of one-eighth or a quarter of an acre of cane, if they be not able to join them, can have at home a small wooden mill and a boiler; and the neighbours of more humble means may unite at home, and assist each other in preparing the sugar for the use of their families throughout the year. Such and similar establishments the united companies might, in time, be enabled to form; and, while labouring to effect this great good, and to prepare a happy state of existence for the future inhabitants of those extensive waste lands in America, their labour would richly repay them for their capital thus employed, in the increased value of the lands.

The plan proposed will be comprised under the following heads:— That chartered societies be organized, in different parts of the civilized world, uniting their interest and plan of operation in the common aim of abolishing slavery amongst those people who profess a belief in revealed religion; that their principal endeavour be to promote a general and consistent system of education, founded on the basis of practical religion and useful knowledge, and likewise to carry on agricultural occupations in the West Indies and in particular parts of the continent of America; that the societies endeavour to obtain, from the governments of Europe and America, first, a settled plan for effectually preventing the slave-trade, by equally contributing towards establishing a permanent force—say from 30 to 40 vessels—to cruise from the coast of Madagascar to the river Gambia or Senegal, which shall be considered as neutral, and possessing equal power over all vessels frequenting those seas in peace as well as in war; secondly, to have a period fixed when slavery shall cease in Europe as well as in the continent of Americas and its dependencies; thirdly, to promote the general system of transporting criminals to the West Indies and to certain parts of America, by entering into suitable arrangements with the different governments principally concerned; fourthly, to obtain from the different governments of America and Europe such regulations as may tend to promote the emigration of white population to America; fifthly, to obtain such privileges, from the different governments, in favour of the societies, as may be consistent with their laws and policy: such as that of remitting a reasonable portion of duties on the introduction of stores and other necessaries for the use of their establishments, as well as on all produce raised by them, and imported in any place for consumption.*

In order to carry these objects into full operation, it is proposed, That the united companies do purchase suitable lands in the colonies of their respective governments, and in such other countries as may be deemed advantageous to the genius and pursuits of the emigrants. That their object be simply to choose a good location in the vicinity of some populous district, and on the borders of a navigable stream, to establish plantations for raising such produce as may be most lucrative and suitable to the interest and object of the societies.

That their establishments be conducted as much upon the system of a penitentiary as is possible, and that order, system, and practical religion be the discipline and main objects amongst the inmates.

---

* By this means, every individual in Europe, as well as in America, will virtually contribute towards the emancipation of slaves; and the planter will not then complain that the European does not, and is not willing to, bear a part in pecuniary sacrifices. He will, no doubt, ask, What compensation is this to me, when the united societies are alone benefited? But the planter must bear in mind, that the effect of the system adopted by the companies operates to increase the value of his real estate when the general emancipation takes place; and that, if these measures be not adopted, the property of the slave-owner will daily decrease, from the spirit of insubordination which must naturally augment among the slaves. Whereas, by enforcing such measures, the services of the slave are secured to the master up to a certain period, at the expense of the governments to which the colonies may belong. But if the planter choose to avail himself of the privileges granted in favour of the societies, nothing can prevent him from joining in the same interest, and from partaking in the same advantages.

That the children be educated in a separate establishment, and that their education be continued to the age of *twenty-one*. That it principally consist, first, in training the mind to make the will of God the main-spring of action; not to be drawn from moral books, but from the pure word of the Bible, with the contents of which they must be made familiar; *not for faith only, but for the regulation of their conduct.* Secondly, that they have an insight into the principles of the natural sciences, in order that they may have a practical knowledge of agriculture or some other useful profession, upon a scientific principle.*

That at the age of twenty-one, the children thus educated be considered free, but should any of them not possess the means of beginning the world, he may with his wife be allowed to serve the proprietors for a term of years, and his services shall be considered as an equivalent for a small plantation, of from two to ten acres, at which time the proposed new system of agriculture will be considered to be fully established. Such is the plan offered to the consideration of those who are actuated by principle, and not by feeling, and who are willing to do more than meet and pass condemnatory resolutions. Stir yourselves and ask the aid of God: He desires that you may do his will, fear not the magnitude of the undertaking, nothing is too great with the divine assistance, everything is so without it. The plan may appear great in viewing the result, but in reality the means are simple. At its commencement, however, it may only be traced, and, like a skeleton map, the divisions be filled up by degrees. The principle on which the plan is founded, is both natural and feasible, for what can be more simple than a system of education? without it nothing can be effected. By commencing a system of improvement, founded on the solid basis of practical religion, you will attack prejudice with the only weapon likely to subdue it; you will then avert the vengeance of retributive justice; and atone by the labours bestowed on succeeding generations, for the cruelties inflicted on their forefathers; and you will then ward off the calamities, with which that hemisphere is threatened, and introduce such a state of society as will be a blessing to it and to the world at large. But the united societies can do no more than endeavour to unite the minds of men in one general plan of operation, for the establishment of small communities,

* This may be objected to by persons who confine education to that class of society called *high*. This heathenish theory has had its reign long enough in all conscience! To their Greek and Latin, their tasteful arts or writings, &c., the poor will give up all pretensions. But, really, the Bible and the book of nature are the patrimony of all men, be they poor or rich. Surely every being who is endowed with the faculty of knowing and of being operated upon by the justice and mercy of his Creator, has an equal right to be made acquainted with them.

where a system of education, consistent with the religion professed, is made general, and a course of agriculture pursued suitable to the soil, climate, and policy of the country. They alone cannot make as great an impression, if the governments do not second their efforts, they should direct their attention to the only means there is of promoting an effective system for improving the rising generation. In this great object the welfare of both Europe and America are inseparably united. The improvement is easy and practicable, particularly in America, by adopting a consistent and useful system of education, where the children of the poor of all classes may be trained to the *practical knowledge* of the precepts which the word of God enjoins, and have a competent knowledge of nature, until the age of twenty-one.

This system will be found to be as natural and as necessary to the youth, as the air which it breathes. Give the child an opportunity of coming within the influence of the word of God and the secrets of nature, uncontaminated by studies of heathen morality, and he need not apply to the classical scholar to teach him wisdom, taste, or even refinement. Let such a system of education be general, and legislators need not study the Roman codes in order to institute laws for the suppression of crime. Indeed, if the governments of civilized countries would consider their true interest and duty, a general education would occupy their principal attention. To understand, and to be trained to act up to the dictates of the Bible, and the easy and simply knowledge of nature, is, and ought to be, the patrimony of every person. And were this generally the case, there would be less occasion for Sheriffs, Prisons, and Soldiers. Such a system of education may be made general, particularly in tropical climates, with very little expense; nay, one might almost venture to say, that, in process of time, the establishments would be capable of maintaining themselves. This will not appear extravagant, when we reflect that the system of education proposed, is that of teaching by practice and not by theory, and that the student is to remain in the establishment until the age of 21: also, that it is in a climate where clothing will not be expensive, and a soil where an acre of plaintain will maintain 50 persons. I do therefore solemnly call on the British government in particular, and on all the other powers possessing colonies, to enforce the education of the rising generation of blacks on their masters, and to take them under their own *special* superintendence. All the planters in a district may join in appropriating a piece of ground for this purpose; and their slaves, thus educated, will prove better subjects to them. When the general emancipation shall take place, they will find themselves surrounded by well-informed, grateful, people, instead of savage enemies, and what may be lost in the nominal property the planter has in the slaves, will be gained by the increase of the value of real estate. If this, or some other system, preparatory to the emancipation which sooner or later *must take place,* be not commenced by the planters, this appeal, amongst others, will testify against them, and they will stand condemned in the eyes of future generations, for whom they are preparing unspeakable miseries. On the other hand, I will venture to say, to all those in England who, operated upon by mere morbid sensibility, will press for a partial emancipation in their colonies: "Consider that the number of English slaves is very small, when compared with the total, and that the English slaves are not far removed from the African savage in civilization: nay, in many respects, they are more vicious, for they have the vices of the African, and also of the Christian, without their virtues." I will lastly direct their attention to the 28th chap. Of Isaiah, from verse 23 to the end. "Give ye ear, and hear my voice; hearken, and hear my speech. Doth the plowman plow all day to sow? doth he open and break the clods of his ground? When he hath made plain the face thereof, doth he not cast abroad the fitches, and scatter the cummin, and cast in the principal wheat, and the appointed barley, and the rice, in their place? For his God doth instruct him to discretion, *and* doth teach him. For the fitches are not threshed with a threshing instrument, neither is a cart-wheel turned about upon the cummin; but the fitches are beaten out with a staff, and the cummin with a rod. Bread *corn* is bruised; because he will not ever be threshing it, nor break *it with* the wheel of his cart, nor bruise it *with* his horsemen. This also cometh forth from the LORD of hosts, *which* is wonderful in counsel, *and* excellent in working."

Imitate then the works of the Creator! Plough the ground before you sow the seed! Take the pains to cultivate, if you desire to reap good fruit!

To the different powers of Europe, and to the united states of America and Mexico, I will say that the slave-holding countries, if allowed to go on as they have done, besides entailing on future generations immense trouble, will, in a great degree, retard the progress of improvement. It is impossible that the slaves or slave-holding states, can extricate themselves from the thraldom of slavery. It cannot be expected. You must therefore take them under your own tutelage, direct their councils if they will, or force them to the measure if they will not.

I will now in conclusion add, that the like establishments recommended in the West Indies and in America, may with little expense and trouble be formed on the coast of Africa: not in the latitude of Sierra Leone, or Liberia, but more towards the North or South of the line. I will rather make the colonization system insinuate itself by degrees upon the tropical latitudes, than plunge into them at once. Numerous establishments may be commenced on small scale, indeed, at first, under the protection of the established naval forces. When the colonies are in a prosperous train, and the slave-trade completely at an end, the vessels may be employed in transporting such free families as may wish to remove to the African settlements. There are many ways to induce them to emigrate. It may be done by a grant of land, or any other allurement which the policy of the governments may think fit to offer. By this means that huge continent of Africa, which has for so many years baffled the efforts of the whites, in the repeated attempts to civilize its inhabitants, will yield to Missionaries of their own colour. They, with the Bible in their hand, will exclaim to their countrymen, "Behold the descendants of those whom you, by your inhumanity, forced from their homes to slavery, but grieve not, 'You have thought it for evil, but God meant it for good.' We have been carried as slaves, and we served as slaves under the yoke of idolatry, superstition, and ignorance, but we are no more so. This blessed book has secured our freedom; those who enslaved us, operated upon by its influence, made us first worthy of our freedom, and have now broken our chains. They have sent us to offer it to your acceptance." By this means, the present generation may, if it please, secure in the most effectual manner, the civilization of the benighted sons of Africa, and justify the ways of God to man. It will clearly demonstrate that, although the original slave traders were acted upon by selfish motives, to the condemnation of their souls, they were nevertheless made instruments of the hand of providence, "to bring about his work, his strange work;" and to show that the Lord, by his inscrutable ways, advances mankind to the light of revelation, from one providential step to another; that the Creator leads his free agent man, with a cord of love towards himself, to that state where the influence of his word will indisputably reign alike in the hearts of men; when God will be all in all, when he will be one and his name one.

Mills, Jowett, and Mills, Bolt-court, Fleet-street.

TEN DOLLARS REWARD.

 **R**AN AWAY from the sub-scriber, a *Negro man* na-med *Charles*, and a *Negro wo-man* named *Dorcas*. The man is about forty years old, and the woman thirty-eight. The man is very black—about five feet nine inches in height,— with the African marks on his face of his native country. The woman is about five feet nine inches, and rather thick set. Any person returning them shall receive the above reward. **HENRY W. MAXEY.**

Cedar Point, March 4. 1w10

Advertisement from the *Jacksonville Courier*, 16 April 1835

ABOUT THE EDITOR

CHRIS MONACO is an independent scholar and documentary film-maker. He holds a Master of Fine Arts degree from the University of South Florida and has received awards from the Florida Historical Society and the Florida Trust for Historic Preservation. He is a contributor to *The Florida Historical Quarterly* and *American Jewish History*.